# Come As You Are

# Come As You Are

Betty Southard
& Marita Littauer

BETHANY HOUSE PUBLISHERS
MINNEAPOLIS, MINNESOTA 55438

*Come As You Are*


Cover design by the Lookout Design Group



Published by Bethany House Publishers
A Ministry of Bethany Fellowship International
11400 Hampshire Avenue South
Minneapolis, Minnesota 55438
www.bethanyhouse.com

Printed in the United States of America by
Bethany Press International, Minneapolis, Minnesota 55438

ISBN 1–55661–017–3

To Armené,
whose enthusiasm for the topic
was a constant source of encouragement
and whose life is a living example
of how to *Come As You Are*.

BETTY SOUTHARD

To my e-mail list,
without your support and
instantaneous input, this book
probably would not have happened
and certainly would not have the
variety and validity it now has.
Thank you!

MARITA LITTAUER

BETTY SOUTHARD is a dynamic communicator with twenty-five years of Bible teaching plus a Master of Theology degree from Fuller Seminary. She is the Minister of Caring for the Hour of Power (Crystal Cathedral Ministries) and has published one other book. She and her husband have three grown daughters and live in California.

MARITA LITTAUER is a professional speaker and author as well as the president of CLASServices. *Come As You Are* is her eighth book. She has been teaching on the Personalities for over fifteen years. She and her husband live in New Mexico.

---

Both Betty and Marita are available for speaking engagements. They can be reached through

CLASServices, Inc.
PO Box 66810
Albuquerque NM 87193
800-433-6633
www.classervices.com

# Contents

# Desperately Seeking Spirituality

# 1

BETTY WAS NAVIGATING THE AISLES of her favorite Christian bookstore when she almost collided with a woman whose arms were overflowing with books. Glancing from the books to her face, she couldn't help but notice that the woman was in a state of confused indecision. Introducing herself, Betty asked if she could be of help. Sharon seemed pleased to have some guidance and said, "I don't know which book to choose. I am looking for a daily devotional."

Betty looked at the books in her arms and was amazed to see that she had picked up everything from Emilie Barnes to Oswald Chambers. No wonder she was confused.

"Tell me what kind of devotional you want," Betty asked.

"Something that feels warm and comforting, but not just fluff. I need something that will make me stretch spiritually, too."

Betty looked over her selections with her, comparing the styles and messages of each author to Sharon's own needs. Finally she eliminated all but the one she felt sure she would like. After thanking Betty profusely, she went to make her purchase.

## Seeking Spirituality

How many times have you stood in a bookstore, wanting to find a tool to help you meet God in a daily setting? How many times have you felt so overwhelmed by the sheer number of books that you left without buying anything? Have you ever chosen something so alien to who you are that it doesn't take long before you throw it down in despair? Have you ever wondered which devotional book, Bible study, or even Bible version you would be most likely to stick with and enjoy? No wonder! It has been said that there are nearly 5,000 new Christian books published every year!

Both Christian and general trade bookstores are filled with a confusing selection of titles designed to address our spiritual needs. There are all kinds of Bibles: the various translations; study Bibles; devotional Bibles; women's, men's, and children's Bibles; recovery Bibles; large-print Bibles; little pocket Bibles; there is even a *One Minute Bible*. There are prayer journals, notebooks, and a variety of books on how to pray. There are daily devotional books for every kind of need and stage of life. Some are filled with sweet stories that give us an inspirational uplift for the day. Others are more like a workbook, taking us through a standard set of steps, which, if followed, will lead us to God. Some are deep and hard to understand.

Take a look at the Spiritual Life section of the store. Here are authors who provide specific instructions for connecting to God. Yet while many of these authors have a good reputation and are nationally known, their advice may contradict one another, even though it is presented as the only way or the best way. It becomes confusing as to what is the "right" way to get closer to God, and we may become unsure of our ability to discern truth from error.

Is there a right way to seek spirituality?

God created each of us unique, yet the prepared spiritual life programs treat us as if we will all seek God in the same way and respond to him in the same way. The truth is that we each view life from a slightly different perspective, including the way we read and study God's Word.

As we speak to various groups around the country representing numerous denominations, we have found that many people have tried the prescribed plans and failed. Not only do they not feel closer to God, they actually feel further away! After hearing testimony after testimony of how a specific devotional system has been effective for many others, people feel that the failure of that particular system in their lives must be due to a personal deficiency rather than the fault of the tried-and-true method. Since it didn't work for them, they feel God does not approve of them or that they are not good enough.

In their book *Experiencing God,* Henry T. Blackaby and Claude V. King tell us, "God pursues a continuing love relationship with you that is real and personal." They go on to say, "This is probably the most important aspect of knowing and doing the will of God."[1] God extends the invitation to us: *Meet with me. Get to know me*. This is a theme repeated throughout Scripture. It is as if he says, *I love you and want to be your friend and guide*. While God repeatedly invites us into his presence, accepting that invitation is our choice alone. God always waits with open arms. He calls to us, reaches out to us, but never forces himself on us.

Amy told us about her experiences with seeking spirituality:

> I had a very close relationship with God from the time I was just a little girl. I was taught: "God loves you; God loves you; God loves you." I talked to him even when I was on the playground, just as though he was there on the swing with me (which he was)!
>
> When I was thirty-one, I invited Jesus into my heart as my

Lord and Savior. For a year I was on my own with God. Then I was exposed to the Word through a Bible study group. It was a small group of well-meaning women, who loved God and were committed to teaching me how to be his disciple. I was in love with God and wanted so much to please him. I lapped up their teaching like a hungry kitten at a bowl of milk.

Three years later, lonely and sad, Amy wrote these words in her journal:

My Father, do you remember a long time ago, when I used to sit at your feet and lay my head on your lap? I would cry then, Father, because I hurt, and you would put your warm, strong hands on my head and just stroke my hair. You never told me to stop my tears. You never were too busy. You always waited until I had cried every last tear. I felt your concern and love so deeply. You never even had to speak your love—I just knew it. And I knew you would take care of me.

And do you remember, even further back, when I was the skinniest kid in town—a tomboy with pigtails and scarred knees? Remember how I'd stop right in the middle of the playground and ask you a question? Sometimes I'd wait for an answer, and sometimes not. But I always knew you were there. I never even considered you might not be. I just knew you were always delighted in just who I was.

It was so easy then, Father. Because, you see, I never pictured you in a throne room. I never imagined I would have to get myself ready to talk to you. I never knew there was a proper way to approach you. You were just my "Daddy," my "Abba." I could curl up on your lap whenever I wanted to. I didn't realize then that I should never start my day without talking first to you. I hadn't heard that I should never cry to you because that would be "murmuring and complaining." You see, I never understood that there were certain rules involved in speaking to you.

So I listened to those who taught the rules and procedures,

> and I learned them well. I even shared them with others, often proudly expounding my new knowledge: "This is what you need to do—try this; begin in this way."
>
> But do you know what, Father? I miss you. I miss you! I want to put my head on your lap again and feel your hug. Yes, I know you're seated on a beautiful throne, but couldn't I just burst into that throne room when I want to share something exciting? All those rules have filled my head with so much knowledge and made me proud. Now I can impress people with how well I know the rule book. But I don't want that, Father. I want you! I just want to be your daughter again. I love you, Abba.

Amy's hunger for an intimate relationship with God comes from that place deep within each of us that Pascal called the "God-shaped vacuum." That longing to be known, loved, accepted, heard, and valued for who we are. A relationship that is not dependent on what we do. But, unfortunately, many have never experienced that relationship personally, and thus look to other people for answers.

The world is seeking answers, and everyone is hoping to find it in spirituality. Secular magazines are dedicating whole issues to spiritual things. *Self* magazine's cover headline blares: "Your Spiritual Life."[2] Underneath are such subtopics as: "The Guide to Peace of Mind: A Meditation Chart"; "Workouts to Soothe the Soul"; "What Fasting Does for Your Mind and Body"; "Why Is Buddhism So Hip? Spirituality for Beginners"; "The Ten Commandments: What They Mean Today"; and in small print: "and of course, 'Angels.' "

But this is not something only women's magazines are addressing. Others are speaking to this hunger. Diverse publications from weekly newsmagazines to the *Wall Street Journal* are printing numerous articles on spirituality.[3] Newspaper editors and guest columnists write about their own spiritual experiences or searches (see William F. Buckley's *Nearer My God*). We hear spirituality being discussed on talk radio. We find television newsmagazines and talk shows interviewing and reporting on topics such as "life after death" and "finding inner peace." Many are asking questions concerning faith. Larry King often interviews well-known ministers, plying them with tough questions. We can almost hear the hunger in these people's voices as they seek to find answers to life's big questions. Psychic networks on the Internet and over telephone lines promise to put one in touch with "god." Many bestselling books on the market have titles like *Conversations With God* or *Simple Abundance*. There is a real hunger for meaning in life. Yet with all our searching, few have found real answers.

The search continues. The editors at *Entrepreneur* magazine picked fourteen top trends for 1997, one of which was spirituality. "As a backlash to the materialistic '80s, and the austere early '90s, spirituality is making a comeback," they stated. An *Utne Reader* survey found that the majority of people surveyed thinks the most significant issue facing this country is "spiritual and moral decay."

Pollster George Gallup says that our society is coming to the end of its emotional resources. "When that happens," he says, "people turn to God." Indeed, 96 percent of U.S. adults say they believe in God (or a universal spirit). But this increase in interest perhaps should be called "spirituality lite." Religion is big in Hollywood as long as Scripture isn't involved, states Paul McGuire in the *Christian American Newsletter*. This is evidenced by all the superficial references to God in popular music, TV shows about heaven and angels, etc. We want comfort; we want to believe in a benevolent God. We want someone to take care of us, but we don't want to have to change our ways.

Yet all this seeking isn't filling the heartfelt need in people. New Age writer Mark Matousek was quoted in *Context* as saying,

> I've come to detest the word spirituality. After years of working in the so-called spiritual community, and writing about the path for a living, I've OD'd on sacred lingo, terms such as "mystical," "enlightenment," "awakening." I'm saddened by how

> empty these words sound to me now, reduced to clichés through overexposure. I'm struck by what these words have come to hide and falsify in our scramble for higher consciousness.[4]

If seeking spirituality seems so elusive, why bother? Will entering such a relationship make any difference in our daily lives?

Betty has had many opportunities to discover the importance of an intimate relationship with God:

> As the mother of three daughters, I was often driven to my knees before the Lord. Particularly as they began dating. I prayed them in and out of many relationships. Well, prayed, cajoled, nagged, argued, lectured, demanded, punished, counseled—whatever worked.
>
> I remember one very destructive and controlling relationship in which one of our daughters was involved. I had exhausted all avenues to derail that relationship, including sending our daughter to Australia for summer missions. Nothing worked! Besides being very frightened, I was becoming angry with God. If it was so clear to me how destructive this relationship was, why didn't he do something about it! My prayer time became more of a venting of my fear and frustration. During one of these times, after a particularly upsetting phone call, I lay exhausted before the Lord. I was at my wit's end. In my silence (finally), and exhaustion, I began to sense his presence. I recalled Jeremiah 29:11. It was as if the Lord was quoting it to me, saying, "I know the plans I have for Kristi," says the Lord. "Plans for good and not for evil. To give her a future and a hope." He continued, "Will you trust her to me? Let go of trying to break up this relationship; release her to me."
>
> "But, Lord," I argued, "she isn't listening to me, and I don't think she is listening to you, either." All kinds of fears and doubts surrounded me. This was my precious, tender, beautiful daughter. She means well. She has told me she is sure that she can help and fix this young man. "O Lord, she is so naïve and trusting."

All I heard in response was "Let go; trust me. Let go; trust me."

"I want to, Lord, but how?" I cried. Everything I had tried so far hadn't worked. The situation was eating me up internally. My insides twisted and turned every time I thought of her. I was losing sleep over the "what ifs." With every phone call from her college dorm, I was thrown into an emotional turmoil. I was so wrapped up in fears over her situation that I was unable or unwilling to rejoice in the good things happening in the lives of our other daughters. I really needed to release Kristi to the Lord, but I was so afraid. I knew that God would not overrule her free will. But I, as a fool, would rush in where angels fear to tread. I didn't mind using every trick I could think of to make her see things my way. If I stopped intervening, and the Holy Spirit didn't intervene, what might happen? These were the thoughts and emotions engulfing me that day as I felt the hopelessness of the situation.

But gently, patiently, tenderly, God simply kept repeating in my mind, *I know the plans I have for Kristi, plans for good and not for evil. To give her a future and a hope.*

I began to cling to this promise, and finally one day I surrendered Kristi to the Lord. From that time forward, every time the fears or doubts flooded my soul, with every phone conversation, I simply repeated God's promise internally. When I was tempted to "advise" or intervene, I felt his gentle admonition: "Trust me; let go."

Slowly, but surely, I found my stomach unknotting, the fears subsiding, and the anger fading. Moment by moment, then day by day, I was able to let go, inch by inch. After a few weeks I was startled to realize that Kristi wasn't consuming my thoughts twenty-four hours a day anymore. The situation still hadn't changed outwardly, but inwardly I was learning to let go and trust.

Eventually God did, in his time, finally give Kristi the wisdom and strength to break off that relationship. But it wasn't because of any effort on my part. In fact, I began to discover that the more I tried to control the situation, the less freedom God seemed to have to work. God used Kristi's situation to teach me a lesson that has had a profound and lasting impact in my life. Much of that lesson was learned as I set aside time to read the Bible and listen for God's voice consistently. Regular communication with God continues to be the key to my trusting God with the unfixable situations in my life.

Reaching this point in my life didn't happen overnight. I didn't discover some "magical" formula that, once I followed it, guaranteed instant success and holiness. For years, though, I lived under the misconception that there was a magical formula out there. All I needed to do was discover it, follow its simple steps, and voilà! all my problems would be solved. Believing this myth led me down some very strange paths indeed.

Both of us have had experiences while seeking spirituality that made us feel as though we were wrong. Along the way we have met others who also longed for an intimate relationship with God, but who also felt like there must be something wrong with them. It seems that at some point most of us have felt like a second-class citizen in the kingdom of God.

Through the years, like perhaps you have, we have listened to others share how real God was to them, how personal their daily devotional time was, how he never failed to speak to them with specific guidance and direction for each day. Independently, we wondered why we weren't always having the same experiences. We listened carefully. We asked lots of questions. Then we would, once again, try to follow the formula, thinking that perhaps this time we would get it right—right enough that God would meet us, speak to us, and, yes, we would find that deep intimacy with him for which we longed. But it rarely happened. We'd try and try again . . . and, once more, rise from our quiet time disappointed, discouraged, wondering what was wrong with us.

Yes, there were times when God seemed very near and real. Times when we did hear his voice and sense his presence. But those times seemed more likely to happen for Betty when she was least expecting it. Times when she was walking in the woods or on the ocean beach. Sometimes it would be in the midst of conversation with a friend or while listening to a sermon, tape, or seminar. God has often used music to bring Betty into his presence and send her in new directions.

Marita found that some of her best times with God were during long, boring drives. Unlike Southern California, where Betty lives, New Mexico is full of long, straight highways with few cars on the road and big open stretches. There, with her mind free to focus on the needs at hand, Marita often hears God's specific direction or answer. New Mexico is also filled with an amazing abundance of natural beauty. At the foot of a waterfall, on the top of a snow-covered mountain, in a lava tube or a small cave gurgling with hot spring water, or even in the sunshine on the tennis court, Marita is filled with awe of God's majesty. Here she worships God and praises his greatness. Recently Marita was at a conference where the music was so spectacular that it filled her with God's presence. While not gifted vocally, she sang praises to God with everything she had in her because the music was so moving.

We have each enjoyed the blessings of those special connections with God, but they didn't happen during the "prescribed" daily quiet or devotional time that we were taught each growing Christian "should" have. Was this okay? Could we meet God outside of a daily devotional time? Did it count?

These are some of the questions we want to answer as we share with you the discoveries we have made. Discoveries in the lives of others, which have shown us that the God who made us each so different delights to meet us according to how he has made us. As we begin to realize how unique we are, we are set free to understand that our process of meeting him will also be unique, fitted specifically for us, and may or may not fit the popular plan.

We believe that God desires to connect with each of us individually. This book will share the experiences of many people, giving examples and ideas to help you find your own personal way of experiencing God—a way that fills that empty void and meets your needs. There are many ways to experience God, ways that span the differences in personalities, lifestyles, and ages.

In preparation for writing this book, we took more than five hundred surveys from people all across the country. Surveys to find out if there really is a spiritual hunger out there. Are people connecting with God in a way that makes a difference in their daily lives? What frustrations are they facing in seeking a more intimate relationship with God? What keeps us from setting aside time to meet with God each day? Are there ways in which we can meet with God in spite of our time constraints? Is it worth the extra trouble? What have people found that works for them? Do different personalities truly experience God differently?

The response we got convinced us that, yes, there is a deep longing to be regularly connected with God in a relational, personal way. There is a lot of frustration and many misconceptions about how to do this. And yes, personalities do experience God in different ways. We found that those who understood why their reactions were different from others—and had come to accept themselves as God created them—were far more likely to have found a meaningful way to connect with God, a way that worked for them. A way that may not correspond to the "myths" they had formerly believed. These myths and misunderstandings are what we will dispel in our next chapter.

# Myths and Misunderstandings

# 2

IN A EUROPEAN CITY THERE ONCE LIVED a famous suit maker called Hans the Tailor. When an influential entrepreneur arrived in the city, he immediately went to Hans's shop and requested a suit. But when he went to pick up his suit, he found that one sleeve twisted this way and the other that way. One shoulder bulged out and the other caved in.

The poor man pulled and struggled, until finally, wrenched and contorted, he managed to make his body fit the strange configuration of the suit. Not wanting to cause a scene, he thanked the tailor, paid his money, and caught the bus to his hotel.

A passenger on the bus stared at the businessman's odd appearance for a long time, and finally asked if Hans the Tailor had made the suit. "Yes, indeed," replied the businessman.

"Amazing!" exclaimed the passenger. "I knew Hans was a great tailor, but I had no idea he could make a suit to fit so perfectly someone as deformed as you!"[1]

## Myths

And that is what many myths have done! They have taken people and pushed and shoved until they were wrenched and contorted, and then someone proudly announces, "See how they fit!" In our attempt to fit all personalities into a one-size-fits-all devotional time, we have distorted the natural gifts and abilities that God has uniquely programmed into each of us. And we have created spiritual misfits. Onlookers have gazed on these deformed people and decided that if that is what "spirituality" looks like, they will pass.

### The Right Way

Perhaps you, too, have tried to stuff yourself into some form that another has said was the "right" way to connect with God. Maybe some of the forms that have paralyzed others have also kept you from connecting with God. Let's look at some that were shared with us.

### I Don't Know Theology

Ann confessed, "In my life, I was afraid to read the Bible because I thought, or got the idea, that I would translate it wrong. I still get scared of that."

Many people have been taught that they are not capable of truly interpreting the Bible for themselves. This has caused them to feel unable to trust that what they might glean from reading the Scriptures could really be God speaking directly to them.

### I Don't Measure Up

Kathleen Norris stated in *Christianity Today,* "I have lately realized that what went wrong for me in my Christian upbringing is centered in the belief that one had to be dressed up, both outwardly and inwardly, to meet God."[2] How many of us have felt that our personality, way of dressing, or being, in life has kept us from being accepted by God?

Mary was raised a Christian but no longer thinks of herself as one. She compares her thoughts about God to her thoughts about her father, who died more than twenty years ago: "I think he would be proud of me, but I always feel he would say I could do better. I think God is like that." Mary believes the myth that she isn't measuring up to what God wants her to be; therefore she cannot connect with him. Consequently, rather than try and fail, Mary has given up on God. Our own perceptions of what God or others expect of us often cause us to give up even before we begin. Our relationships within our families, or perhaps with people who are critical of us, have kept many of us from believing that God can love us unconditionally.

## I Can't Get Up at the Crack of Dawn

Others believe that in order to have meaningful times with the Lord they must get up early in the morning. They believe reading the Bible must be done for a prescribed length of time and that they need to find something special every day in their reading to make it count.

## That Doesn't Work for Me

Another barrier is the comparison of our quiet time with God to that of others, particularly those who proudly tell us how God meets and directs them every day. Many times Betty has felt left out as another friend shares the ways that God speaks personally to her each day through her Bible reading.

Anita was taught that there were certain formulas to be followed. These included how much Scripture should be read each day, the amount of time spent reading, and how prayer time should be structured. Of course, depending on the source, she even got conflicting messages on these formulas.

### I Hate to Write

Many quiet-time experts suggest that we write out our prayers, and there are some very popular books that encourage us to do this. This approach has been helpful to some people. Others say that journalizing is an integral part of a devotional hour. (Both of us have tried this method but found it to be more discipline than devotion.)

### I Just Don't Have Time

Busyness is another barrier to spending time with God. Just how much time must you spend in Bible reading, prayer, meditation, and journalizing? Is there a certain amount that is the key to success? If you don't have a consistent daily time with the Lord, are you still loved and accepted by him? These are questions I puzzled over with my friend Connie as we talked about our own struggle in finding the "right" way to connect with God.

## Misunderstandings

Connie stated, "Our conversation this morning helped me think about my assumptions about devotional life and Bible study. I have bobbed on the surface of the 'cares of the day in my world' or fastened an anchor to some 'formula' and had the anchor line snap with the first serious turbulence. Aside from my faulty approaches, my assumptions set me up for failure."

### "Shoulds" and "They"

What assumptions, faulty approaches, or false expectations have set you up for failure? In chapter 1, Amy spoke of the "shoulds" that turned her close relationship with God as a child into a meaningless, frustrating experience as she followed the "rules and regulations" of well-meaning Christian friends. She said,

> How intrusive and interfering the "shoulds" are in keeping

me away. I never really looked before at the "shoulds" as being so closely tied to "them." I always thought "they" were speaking for God. I guess if you really think about it, there are no shoulds in God's vocabulary, for each directive is a pure commandment. "Just do it!" he always says. It is "they" who add the "should." What a freeing thought. It visually separates God from the shoulds and clarifies the purity of his love and commandments.

Amy is being set free to find the way to "crawl back up into God's lap" and meet him at the point of her need. Not as a careless tomboy again, but as the unique maturing daughter he made her to be.

## Excuses

But it is not only the myths we believe that keep us from our divine appointments with God. There are a million reasons or, in reality, excuses why we don't. Here are just a few that we gathered from our surveys.

### False Expectations

"The peace and harmony I need with a young family have not allowed me time for this." Then Mary added, "My home church group is too full of people telling me how things should be done, and that has discouraged me." Many young women experience frustration and discouragement. The expectations that they assume others are placing on them often add to their own sense of guilt. Just coping with the demands of young children and trying to keep their heads above water is about all many young mothers can handle.

### Too Busy, Too Tired

"I am so busy doing my Christian duty, that I'm spending my time with God in my hours of Christian service. I am too tired from caring for others to take care of myself" was the reason Mary Ellen of Long

Beach, California gave. Sometimes it seems easier to keep busy "doing" Christian work than to spend time listening to God and finding his direction.

## Not Applicable

Jane responded with the excuse that "if it were applicable and meaningful to my everyday life, if it brought peace and inspiration, I might try it, but honestly, I lack interest." Interestingly enough, her survey said she had never really tried to have any personal devotional time. There may be many different reasons why one has not even attempted to spend time alone with God.

## Need More Information

Lily said, "If I don't have a devotion time, it is because I get up two seconds before I need to leave the house. I feel distant from God, lonely. My Bible isn't near my bed, and when I get up, I forget. I lack needed information." She gives several reasons, but what is really the truth? What may lie behind the excuses that we give? Is Lily afraid that if she takes time to meet with God, he may make demands on her life? Is she feeling distant and lonely because God has abandoned her? Or has she distanced herself from him? How much trouble can it be to place her Bible by her bed, if she really wants to spend time reading it? What kind of information does she need?

## Fear of Failure

Marcia from Ventura honestly shared her feelings when asked what keeps her from finding time for God. "I've been wanting to do this for a while," she said, "but somehow I'm afraid I'm not worthy or I might not understand." She also shared that a previous bad experience has made her cautious. "I'm afraid I'll find a Bible study group of old 'biddies' who are only there to gossip. I experienced this a long time ago, and I felt very uncomfortable. I said silently, 'Forget this! This is not for me.' Yet I still long for a meaningful relationship with God." All through her survey we could hear her heart cry for something more in her spiritual life. The idea that God wanted to connect with her personally seemed to be unimaginable. She had many other reasons: "I have trouble finding time after work. I don't know how to begin. I feel embarrassed that when I try to talk to God [on her five-minute drive to work] I get distracted and it comes out wrong. Like I'm always begging for help. I get embarrassed."

## Hates Routine

Judy candidly admitted, "I'm not at all structured. I rarely do anything routinely. With three businesses, eight children, and twenty-one grandchildren, time is a problem. I'm not a good reader, and the one book I really do not read much is my Bible. I'm ashamed to say that. I read it at Bible study and read a lot pertaining to it. But I really rarely read the Bible itself."

## Not Interesting, Hard to Understand

Sandy's reason was more creative: "My husband doesn't want me to get up before him in the morning. I'm too tired at night." While Lucy said, "I find it difficult to stay interested in what I'm reading," Andrea wanted a "quiet, comfortable place to go." Dottie, who is single, stated, "I found the Bible hard to read and understand. I was in a Bible study class that would always show women as doormats, not 'people,' unless they had a husband to serve."

## I Forget

"We all have our ups and downs. I find when I'm up and life is good, I forget to pray. When down, I never forget to ask God for help! Therefore, my time with God is more regular when things are tough, and somehow I would rather have things going well than spend time with God" was Donna's assessment of her situation.

### Makes No Difference

"I've tried it before, but it didn't seem to make any difference in my life," declared Liz. Many other women expressed similar feelings. Do any of these excuses sound familiar to you? What has kept you from spending time with God?

### Honest Objections

Perhaps Norma from Indiana summed it up best when she listed the following reasons for not having a regular quiet time:

1. Letting other things come first.
2. Not having materials that inspire me or help me to understand the Bible and its meaning for today.
3. Not having a planned devotional book to use.
4. Not a reader because I find it hard to retain what I read.

In a footnote, she said, "I hope this doesn't sound like I am making excuses. I am just being honest."

## Deep Desires

Honesty is what we asked for, and honesty is what we got. Yet in each response we detected an undercurrent of desire for time alone with God. People really long for a personal connection with God. Even the creators of Hallmark cards realize this. One of their spokespersons recently stated, "The closer we get to the millennium, the more we see that spirituality is something important to people."[3]

## Finding Joy

We have found personally that in years past when we sat down to "dutifully" read the Bible and pray, we often felt like many of the women surveyed have felt. But when we allowed the freedom of who

God made us to be to shape our time with God, we discovered the joy of wanting to meet with God and spend time with him. This time may be through a structured Bible study group. It may be through individual reading or written prayers. But for our personality type, we have found that, more often than not, the traditional methods of connecting with God were not what brought us closer to him. One day one approach seemed appropriate. The next day, depending on our needs and schedule, something totally different worked for us. This freedom and variety have made the difference in our lives!

## There Is a Way

Is there a way to overcome the time constraints of modern living? Can I find a way to meet with God that will keep me interested? Will God meet me personally, just as I am? We give a resounding YES to these questions. Our surveys show that many women have found the answers, and we want to share them with you. But the key to finding these answers lies in understanding the differences in our personalities. As we discover the freedom to be who God created us to be, we also discover the delight in meeting him right where we are. Our next two chapters uncover the various ways God has made us different and give the keys to understanding who we are individually. As we understand ourselves as well as those around us, we will be set free to connect with God according to the way he made us.

# Divine Differences

# 3

JUST AS WE HAVE SEEN THAT PEOPLE SEEK spirituality for different reasons, they also seek it in different ways. But we also respond to God and approach him differently. Let's look at the fictional Sonshine Church. Do any of the characters sound like you or anyone you know? Pastors and layworkers have said that while the following scenario is exaggerated to make a point, it is "right on" and perhaps even too tame in some instances!

## The Sonshine Church

Sally was new in town and didn't know too many people. Having heard that going to church was a great way to make friends, she began to search for a church with people like herself. One day, on the way to the post office, she saw a sign for a new church that met at the local high school. The sign was bright yellow and had contemporary graphic figures reaching for something. She decided she would visit Sonshine Church.

When Sunday came, Sally dressed in bright casual clothing and headed for the high school auditorium. Since the church was new, the group was fairly small, and everyone was very friendly. There didn't seem to be any of the little cliques she remembered from other churches she'd visited. The service began informally with congregational singing. The song leader wore a polo shirt, and his music selections were unencumbered by tradition. He led the enthusiastic group in fast-paced, upbeat choruses, displayed on the wall with an overhead projector. The people moved to the beat and clapped their hands. After a few songs, they had a brief get-acquainted time, and everyone headed to the back of the auditorium, where coffee and donuts were served. As the music started up again, people took their coffee and headed back to their seats.

A young pastor in shirt-sleeves stood up to preach. It was a short sermon with lots of emphasis on the joy of Jesus and the Christian life. He was a great storyteller, and several times people laughed out loud. This church was different from any other Sally had visited. After the service, everyone invited Sally to join them for lunch at a local restaurant.

That first Sunday at Sonshine Church, Sally knew she had found a new church home. She became a regular attender.

Before long, Sally was in charge of the Birthday Committee and was holding midweek meetings in her home. She cleaned her house, baked cookies, and prepared for each meeting as she would a party with friends. The group praised her for her hospitality and seemed to love her unconditionally. In this nurturing environment, Sally discovered that she needed to know God as these people did.

One Sunday, she went forward and prayed with the pastor. She grew week by week, and her face glowed with the love and joy of Jesus. People at her workplace noticed a difference in Sally, and some of them even joined her on Sundays at Sonshine Church.

A few weeks later, Sally noticed someone new at church who didn't seem to fit in with the group. Being the friendly type, Sally made an effort to greet her. Marianne was older than most of the people who met regularly. She was dressed conservatively and appeared quite reserved. Sally soon discovered that Marianne was the mother of Chuck, one of the young married men in the congregation. Marianne's husband had died recently, and she had moved from the Midwest to live with Chuck and his wife, Candi. She would be able to help with their children. She confided to Sally that since she was obviously older than the rest, she thought God had brought her to this church to be a Titus 2 woman. Not wanting to seem uninformed, Sally acted pleased with this news, then went to her seat and looked up Titus 2—at least she knew it was a book of the Bible!

Marianne was disappointed with the simple church her son and his family attended. But she was glad to see that they were active somewhere. She thought perhaps God also had led her here to organize her grandchildren's daily devotions, using proper children's literature. She would take them to special programs such as Vacation Bible School, held at "real" churches (the traditional ones with a steeple and stained glass windows). Feeling overwhelmed, she cried out to God: "O Lord, I will have my hands full here. There is so much to do at Sonshine Church: so many people who need real teaching and discipline. I could start a study for young women like Sally."

Marianne spent hours at the local Christian bookstore, researching tools her flock would need in their search for spirituality. She lost herself in the commentaries and reference books and was almost late getting home before the children returned from school.

Marge worked in the reference section at the bookstore, and she looked forward to Marianne's visits. Not too many people came in searching for deeper truths. After twenty years at the Deeper Life Bible Bookstore, Marge knew the inventory well and loved to share her knowledge with anyone who would listen. With Marge's help,

Marianne soon had a resource list to recommend to the young women at Sonshine. Marianne and Marge became fast friends. Marge attended the large, traditional brick church downtown, and she invited Marianne to attend organ concerts held there on Saturday nights. Marianne purchased CDs of the organ music to play during her study time.

With her mission clearly defined, Marianne started a Bible study on Tuesday evenings for young working women. First thing, she encouraged them to begin a daily Bible reading program with a scheduled quiet time. After all, how could she lead a Bible study with people who didn't even know their way around the Bible? The group met at Sally's house, since she already had it set up for the Wednesday night meeting. Sally loved to have her house filled with people. Besides, all the cars out front would impress the neighbors with her popularity!

Chuck had met the pastor of Sonshine Church at a business-networking meeting. He sensed that the pastor viewed the church like a business; he didn't talk like the King James Bible, and he had a mission statement. Chuck liked the fact that since the church was new, there were not a lot of meetings to attend. He was a busy man who did not have time for meetings—or guilt over not attending them. Once Chuck became a regular church attender, the pastor put him on the board. Chuck owned his own business and dressed well, showing up every Sunday with a different power tie. He would be an asset to the church. Chuck appreciated the fact that the pastor showed discernment; after all, he had spotted Chuck's leadership skills almost the first day they met. The pastor had primed Chuck and given him a position of power.

Chuck arrived early every Sunday to set up chairs and hook up the sound system. His mother had taught him, at an early age, good organizational skills. Chuck oversaw the offering and made the bank deposits. Everyone looked up to him. His business was booming, which allowed him to build an addition onto his house for his mother, and he was sure God was blessing him because of his good church attendance.

One Sunday, the pastor preached on the power of God's presence in the Christian life. He addressed the fact that with this power the Christian could have a more positive impact in his home and in his community. Chuck liked the concept of power and influence in the community; the pastor's sermon related to him. He also came to realize that what he needed most was to have Jesus in his life. He needed to talk with the pastor. Later that week, he and the pastor met, and Chuck invited Jesus into his heart and life.

Now Chuck looked forward to Sunday services with even greater zeal. The sermons made sense to him, and with the power of the Holy Spirit in his life, he felt even more confident.

Fran was a born follower. She was very happy when Sally joined their team at work. She brightened up the office and, becoming a good friend to Fran, she brightened her life, too. Sally was always cheerful and kept everyone laughing. But one day Fran noticed that Sally seemed to have an extra glow about her. Sure that it must be a new cosmetic or something, Fran asked Sally if she had changed her makeup. Sally shook her head. She was still using the same drugstore brand she'd always used. Puzzled, Fran asked, "Is anything else different?"

"I've met Jesus!" Sally gushed. "Come to church with me!" Sally's energy and enthusiasm put Fran off. She couldn't be bothered with religion and considered her Sundays an important time to catch up on sleep and reading.

While she appeared disinterested, Fran watched Sally. Fran saw Sally pray before lunch, and she heard that others in the office had joined Sonshine Church after attending with Sally. As more of the office staff claimed to be "Christians," Fran felt that the atmosphere at work was more peaceful. There was a friendlier tone, too, which created less stress. Slowly, Fran began to be interested. She asked Sally about services. Before Fran could change her mind, Sally had everything arranged. She would pick her up Sunday morning. "Don't dress up; this is a casual church," Sally said. "I'll take you out to lunch with everyone afterward—my treat!" Sally made it sound too good to refuse.

At Sonshine Church, people seemed pleased to see Fran. They didn't make any demands of her but warmly welcomed her into the group. She liked the coffee and donuts in the middle of the service, too. She went back—Sunday after Sunday. Sally noticed Fran didn't have a Bible, so she went to the Deeper Life Bookstore. Marge thought Sally should buy a burgundy leather volume with cross-references and study notes, and a cover that held a notepad, pen, and highlighter. Sally bought a paperback Modern English paraphrase with pictures, to Marge's disappointment.

Fran was touched by Sally's thoughtful gesture, and she faithfully carried her new Bible to church each Sunday. She was amazed that she could understand what she read and even found that sometimes she read her Bible on her own—not just in church.

One Sunday, the pastor preached on John 14:27: "I am leaving you with a gift—peace of mind and heart! And the peace I give isn't fragile like the peace the world gives. So don't be troubled or afraid" (TLB). His words touched her heart, and she underlined them in her Bible. She liked the idea of a gift—it reminded her of Sally's gift. Peace of mind and heart, and the possibility of not being troubled or afraid, were intriguing to her. At the end of the sermon, the pastor asked people to come forward to invite Christ into their life. Fran didn't move. The thought of being seen in front of everyone frightened her. She hung back and, when almost everyone had left, she lightly touched the pastor's arm and whispered that she wanted to invite Jesus into her life. Sally was elated. She skipped the ritual lunch party and stayed with Fran until she had prayed with the pastor.

From that day on, Fran found daily comfort in the words of the Psalms. Marianne taught her to rewrite them in a journal, using her own name. This brought her great comfort and a feeling of belonging.

She frequently used her Saturdays to drive into the hills with a praise tape playing on the car stereo. She found a favorite spot overlooking a creek. She could sit for hours on a rock reading the Bible Sally had given her and meditating on God's Word, the beauty of nature, and her new life. She often fell into a comfortable sleep, smiling as she rested, knowing that God loved her.

Fran shared with Sally how she was growing. She suggested that Sally try the same techniques. While Sally was very happy for her friend, the thought of sitting on a rock for hours was unthinkable to her. She preferred to spend her Saturdays shopping and listening to cassette tapes between stops. At home, she listened to the contemporary Christian music station, singing along at top volume. She also liked keeping up with news of the artists' lives. While not gifted vocally, Sally felt close to God hearing music with a strong beat and words that related to her life.

Marianne was concerned that Chuck and Candi didn't seem to have a regularly scheduled devotional or study time. How could they expect to raise their children for the Lord if they didn't set a godly example of reading God's Word every day? One night, she brought up her concerns to Chuck and Candi. At her home church, everyone was on the same daily reading program, and all used the same version of the Bible. Marianne thought that since Chuck was on the board at Sonshine, he should practice this himself and then institute the changes for everyone in the church.

Her suggestions were not well received. With their business going so well, Chuck and Candi were both working hard. They were grateful that Marianne could help with the children, but their time with them was minimal and certainly didn't allow for an hour a day for devotions. Between sales calls, Chuck prayed in his car. Sometimes he listened to teaching tapes, from which he gained insights into the Christian life. Candi kept the office radio on a Christian teaching station and enjoyed the snippets she could grasp between projects. The couple often shared with each other what they learned and debated the points on which they did not completely agree. When it was Chuck's turn to teach the midweek study, he carved out time at the office to use his Bible software and found that these were the times he grew the most. He had a specific goal and topic, but his schedule did not often allow for intense research. With Chuck and Candi's active and busy lives, they found that their faith carried them through, even if Marianne was concerned for their spirituality.

## God's Creation

The above story pretty well sums up that people are different. We accept that some people are outgoing optimists and others are more introverted and serious. We know that some people enjoy people and place a high priority on relationships, while others prefer to be alone, uninterrupted by others, so they can focus on the task at hand. While we accept and may even understand these differences, most of us do not realize that these very idiosyncrasies that make us the unique individuals we are also impact how we view God, connect with him, and respond to him.

God made each of us with these differences. For years modern science has been trying to prove that environment creates these variances in people. Yet recent research reinforces what every mother of more than one child can tell you: you were born a unique individual. Science is now saying that our individual personality is part of our genetic makeup. *Life* magazine says,

> In one of the most bitter scientific controversies of the twentieth century—the battle over nature and nurture—a wealth of new research has tipped the scales overwhelmingly toward nature. Studies of twins and advances in molecular biology have uncovered a more significant genetic component to personality than was previously known. Far from a piece of putty, say biologists, my daughter is more like a computer's motherboard; her

> basic personality is hardwired into infinitesimal squiggles of DNA.[1]

This new research confirms what many of us were already sure of: God made us each unique and special. We are not a blank slate upon which society writes its plans for our lives.

## Bible Characters

As we search the Scriptures, we see that the key characters have distinct personalities. As such, they respond to God's influence in their lives differently. Let's look at some of the Bible's important but very different characters.[2]

### Peter

"You are Peter, a stone; and upon this rock I will build my church; and all the powers of hell shall not prevail against it" (Matt. 16:18 TLB).

Peter was known to be brash and impulsive. It is said that he often spoke without thinking.

We may wonder what Jesus saw in Simon that made him greet this potential disciple with a new name: Peter, the rock. Impulsive Peter certainly didn't act like a rock much of the time. But Christ accepted him with his strengths and weaknesses. When Jesus chose his followers, he wasn't looking for models; he was looking for real people. He chose people who could be changed by his love, and then he sent them out to communicate that his acceptance was available to anyone—even to those who often fail.

### Paul

"To me the only important thing about living is Christ, and dying would be profit for me. If I continue living in my body, I will be able to work for the Lord. I do not know what to choose—living or dying. It is hard to choose between the two. I want to leave this life and be with Christ, which is much better, but you need me here in my body" (Phil. 1:22–24 NCV).

No person, apart from Jesus himself, shaped the history of Christianity like the apostle Paul. Even before he was a believer, his actions were significant. His frenzied persecution of Christians following Stephen's death got the church started in obeying Christ's final command to take the gospel worldwide. Paul's personal encounter with Jesus changed his life. He never lost his fierce intensity, but from then on it was channeled for the gospel. Notice the type of activity that surrounded Paul. Words like "intense" and "frenzied" fit the person we know as Paul. He is said to have had a strong personality that was never afraid to face an issue head-on and deal with it.

## Moses

"By faith Moses, when he became of age, refused to be called the son of Pharaoh's daughter, choosing rather to suffer affliction with the people of God than to enjoy the passing pleasures of sin" (Heb. 11:24–25 NKJV).

Moses seemed drawn to what needed to be righted. Throughout his life, he was at his finest and his worst responding to the conflicts around him. Even the burning bush experience was an illustration of his character. Having spotted the fire and having seen that the bush did not burn, he had to investigate. Whether jumping into a fight to defend a Hebrew slave or trying to referee a struggle between two kinsmen, when Moses saw conflict, he reacted. Notice that Moses chose to suffer and had a need to correct the conflicts and investigate.

## Abraham

"And Abram believed God; then God considered him righteous on account of his faith" (Gen. 15:6 TLB).

While Paul is known as a man of action, Abraham is known as a man of faith. Despite his faith, he had a difficult time making decisions. His decision was between setting out with his family for parts unknown and staying right where he was. He had to decide between the security of what he already had and the uncertainty of traveling under God's direction. Through his faith, he did make the right choice, which impacted all of history. However, notice that the difficulty in the decision has to do with security. Abraham usually avoided conflicts, but when they were unavoidable, he allowed his opponent to set the rules for settling the dispute. Because he desired security and peace, under direct pressure he distorted the truth.

---

As we review these brief personality profiles of some of the Bible's best-known characters, we see that they were very different—just like we are. Each of us is unique. However, within our peculiarities there are some common factors. Some of us might be more like Peter, "brash and impulsive," perhaps speaking without thinking. While most people can cite a time when they may have spoken without thinking, for some of us it is a way of life. Some people are more like Paul, having his "fierce intensity." Others are like Moses, feeling "drawn to what needs to be righted." You may feel overwhelmed and frustrated by all the wrongs in the world. Or you may be like Abraham, usually avoiding conflict and desiring peace and security.

These four biblical characters, and those at the fictional Sonshine Church, reflect the four basic personality types we recognize today. Once we understand and accept our own personality type, we can see how God created us and how our personality influences what tools and techniques will be the most effective for us in our search for spirituality.

The personality that is more like Peter (and Sonshine Church's Sally) is what we call the Popular Sanguine. The one that is more like Paul (and Sonshine Church's Chuck and Candi) we call the Powerful

Choleric. Those who are more like Moses (and Sonshine Church's Marianne and Marge) would be the Perfect Melancholy, and the person who is more like Abraham (and Sonshine Church's Fran) is the Peaceful Phlegmatic. While no two of us are exactly alike, most of us do fall into one of these primary profiles.

The names of the personality types are actually from the original Greek words that Hippocrates, a Greek physician and philosopher, first identified over 2,400 years ago as he observed the personalities of those with whom he worked and lived. Since that time, the personality types he developed have been tried and tested, improved and expanded. If you are not familiar with the basic teaching on the personalities, we offer you a brief overview in the next chapter. Additionally, we suggest that you read *Personality Plus, Personality Puzzle,* and *Your Personality Tree.*[3]

# Different Doors

# 4

AS GOD CREATED EACH OF US DIFFERENTLY, he also welcomes us into his presence through different doors. It is like the old saying, "All roads lead to Rome." As long as we know God, through Christ, the exact approach of how we worship and commune with him is not the issue. As we begin to understand our own personality, we can have more freedom in our relationship with him. We can use who he made us to be as an important tool to enter into his presence.

On the following pages, you will find a summary of each of the basic personality types and a personality profile.[1] The summaries will help you to understand each personality type, and the profile will confirm which personality—or personality combination—is yours.

## Your Personality Profile

On page 45, in each of the rows of four words across, place an X in the box in front of the one or two words that most often apply to you. Continue through all forty lines. If you are not sure which word "most applies," ask a spouse or a friend, and think of what your answer would have been when you were a child. Use the following word definitions for the most accurate results.

## Definitions of Strengths

(1) **Adventurous** One who will take on new and daring enterprises with a determination to master them.

**Adaptable** Easily fits in and is comfortable in any situation.

**Animated** Full of life, lively use of hand, arm, and face gestures.

**Analytical** Likes to examine the parts for their logical and proper relationships.

(2) **Persistent** Sees one project through to its completion before starting another.

**Playful** Full of fun and good humor.

**Persuasive** Convinces through logic and fact rather than charm or power.

**Peaceful** Seems undisturbed and tranquil and retreats from any form of strife.

(3) **Submissive** Easily accepts any other's point of view or desire with little need to assert his own opinion.

**Self-sacrificing** Willingly gives up his own personal being for the sake of, or to meet the needs of, others.

**Sociable** One who sees being with others as an opportunity to be cute and entertaining rather than as a challenge or business opportunity.

**Strong-willed** Determined to have one's own way.

(4) **Considerate** Having regard for the needs and feelings of others.

**Controlled** Has emotional feelings but rarely displays them.

**Competitive** Turns every situation, happening, or game into a contest and always plays to win!

# Your Personality Profile

## Strengths

| | | | | |
|---|---|---|---|---|
| 1. | ☐ Adventurous | ☐ Adaptable | ☐ Animated | ☐ Analytical |
| 2. | ☐ Persistent | ☐ Playful | ☐ Persuasive | ☐ Peaceful |
| 3. | ☐ Submissive | ☐ Self-sacrificing | ☐ Sociable | ☐ Strong-willed |
| 4. | ☐ Considerate | ☐ Controlled | ☐ Competitive | ☐ Convincing |
| 5. | ☐ Refreshing | ☐ Respectful | ☐ Reserved | ☐ Resourceful |
| 6. | ☐ Satisfied | ☐ Sensitive | ☐ Self-reliant | ☐ Spirited |
| 7. | ☐ Planner | ☐ Patient | ☐ Positive | ☐ Promoter |
| 8. | ☐ Sure | ☐ Spontaneous | ☐ Scheduled | ☐ Shy |
| 9. | ☐ Orderly | ☐ Obliging | ☐ Outspoken | ☐ Optimistic |
| 10. | ☐ Friendly | ☐ Faithful | ☐ Funny | ☐ Forceful |
| 11. | ☐ Daring | ☐ Delightful | ☐ Diplomatic | ☐ Detailed |
| 12. | ☐ Cheerful | ☐ Consistent | ☐ Cultured | ☐ Confident |
| 13. | ☐ Idealistic | ☐ Independent | ☐ Inoffensive | ☐ Inspiring |
| 14. | ☐ Demonstrative | ☐ Decisive | ☐ Dry Humor | ☐ Deep |
| 15. | ☐ Mediator | ☐ Musical | ☐ Mover | ☐ Mixes Easily |
| 16. | ☐ Thoughtful | ☐ Tenacious | ☐ Talker | ☐ Tolerant |
| 17. | ☐ Listener | ☐ Loyal | ☐ Leader | ☐ Lively |
| 18. | ☐ Contented | ☐ Chief | ☐ Chartmaker | ☐ Cute |
| 19. | ☐ Perfectionist | ☐ Pleasant | ☐ Productive | ☐ Popular |
| 20. | ☐ Bouncy | ☐ Bold | ☐ Behaved | ☐ Balanced |

## Weaknesses

| | | | | |
|---|---|---|---|---|
| 21. | ☐ Blank | ☐ Bashful | ☐ Brassy | ☐ Bossy |
| 22. | ☐ Undisciplined | ☐ Unsympathetic | ☐ Unenthusiastic | ☐ Unforgiving |
| 23. | ☐ Reticent | ☐ Resentful | ☐ Resistant | ☐ Repetitious |
| 24. | ☐ Fussy | ☐ Fearful | ☐ Forgetful | ☐ Frank |
| 25. | ☐ Impatient | ☐ Insecure | ☐ Indecisive | ☐ Interrupts |
| 26. | ☐ Unpopular | ☐ Uninvolved | ☐ Unpredictable | ☐ Unaffectionate |
| 27. | ☐ Headstrong | ☐ Haphazard | ☐ Hard to Please | ☐ Hesitant |
| 28. | ☐ Plain | ☐ Pessimistic | ☐ Proud | ☐ Permissive |
| 29. | ☐ Angers Easily | ☐ Aimless | ☐ Argumentative | ☐ Alienated |
| 30. | ☐ Naïve | ☐ Negative Attitude | ☐ Nervy | ☐ Nonchalant |
| 31. | ☐ Worrier | ☐ Withdrawn | ☐ Workaholic | ☐ Wants Credit |
| 32. | ☐ Too Sensitive | ☐ Tactless | ☐ Timid | ☐ Talkative |
| 33. | ☐ Doubtful | ☐ Disorganized | ☐ Domineering | ☐ Depressed |
| 34. | ☐ Inconsistent | ☐ Introvert | ☐ Intolerant | ☐ Indifferent |
| 35. | ☐ Messy | ☐ Moody | ☐ Mumbles | ☐ Manipulative |
| 36. | ☐ Slow | ☐ Stubborn | ☐ Show-off | ☐ Skeptical |
| 37. | ☐ Loner | ☐ Lords Over Others | ☐ Lazy | ☐ Loud |
| 38. | ☐ Sluggish | ☐ Suspicious | ☐ Short-tempered | ☐ Scatterbrained |
| 39. | ☐ Revengeful | ☐ Restless | ☐ Reluctant | ☐ Rash |
| 40. | ☐ Compromising | ☐ Critical | ☐ Crafty | ☐ Changeable |

**Convincing** Can win you over to anything through the sheer charm of his personality.

(5) **Refreshing** Renews and stimulates or makes others feel good.

**Respectful** Treats others with deference, honor, and esteem.

**Reserved** Self-restrained in expression of emotion or enthusiasm.

**Resourceful** Able to act quickly and effectively in virtually all situations.

(6) **Satisfied** A person who easily accepts any circumstance or situation.

**Sensitive** Intensely cares about others and what happens to them.

**Self-reliant** An independent person who can fully rely on his own capabilities, judgment, and resources.

**Spirited** Full of life and excitement.

(7) **Planner** Prefers to work out a detailed arrangement beforehand for the accomplishment of a project or goal and prefers involvement with the planning stages and the finished product rather than the carrying out of the task.

**Patient** Unmoved by delay, remains calm and tolerant.

**Positive** Knows it will turn out right if he's in charge.

**Promoter** Urges or compels others to go along, join, or invest through the charm of his own personality.

(8) **Sure** Confident, rarely hesitates or wavers.

**Spontaneous** Prefers all of life to be impulsive, unpremeditated activity, not restricted by plans.

**Scheduled** Makes and lives according to a daily plan; dislikes plans being interrupted.

**Shy** Quiet, doesn't easily instigate a conversation.

(9) **Orderly** Having a methodical, systematic arrangement of things.

**Obliging** Accommodating. One who is quick to do it another's way.

**Outspoken** Speaks frankly and without reserve.

**Optimistic** Sunny disposition. One who convinces self and others that everything will turn out all right.

(10) **Friendly** A responder rather than an initiator, seldom starts a conversation.

**Faithful** Consistently reliable, steadfast, loyal, and devoted—sometimes beyond reason.

**Funny** Sparkling sense of humor that can make virtually any story into a hilarious event.

**Forceful** A commanding personality. Someone others would hesitate to take a stand against.

(11) **Daring** Willing to take risks; fearless, bold.

**Delightful** A person who is upbeat and fun to be with.

**Diplomatic** Deals with people tactfully, sensitively, and patiently.

**Detailed** Does everything in proper order with a clear memory of all the things that happened.

(12) **Cheerful** Consistently in good spirits. Promotes happiness in others.

**Consistent** Stays on an even keel emotionally, responding as one might expect.

**Cultured** One whose interests involve both intellectual and artistic pursuits, such as theater, symphony, ballet.

**Confident** Self-assured and certain of own ability and success.

(13) **Idealistic** Visualizes things in their perfect form and has a need to measure up to that standard himself.

**Independent** Self-sufficient, self-supporting, self-confident, and seems to have little need of help.

**Inoffensive** A person who never says or causes anything unpleasant or objectionable.

**Inspiring** Encourages others to work, join, or be involved and makes the whole thing fun.

(14) **Demonstrative** Openly expresses emotion, especially affection, and doesn't hesitate to touch others while speaking to them.

**Decisive** A person with quick, conclusive, judgment-making ability.

**Dry Humor** Exhibits "dry wit," usually one-liners that can be sarcastic in nature.

**Deep** Intense and often introspective with a distaste for surface conversation and pursuits.

(15) **Mediator** Consistently finds him- or herself in the role of reconciling differences in order to avoid conflict.

**Musical** Participates in or has a deep appreciation for music; is committed to music as an art form rather than the fun of performance.

**Mover** Driven by a need to be productive; is a leader whom others follow; finds it difficult to sit still.

**Mixes Easily** Loves a party and can't wait to meet everyone in the room; no one is a stranger.

(16) **Thoughtful** A considerate person who remembers special occasions and is quick to make a kind gesture.

**Tenacious** Holds on firmly, stubbornly, and won't let go until the goal is accomplished.

**Talker** Constantly talking; generally telling funny stories and entertaining everyone; feeling the need to fill the silence in order to make others comfortable.

**Tolerant** Easily accepts the thoughts and ways of others without the need to disagree with or change them.

(17) **Listener** Always seems willing to hear what you have to say.

**Loyal** Faithful to a person, ideal, or job, sometimes beyond reason.

**Leader** A natural-born director, who is driven to be in charge and often finds it difficult to believe that anyone else can do the job as well.

**Lively** Full of life; vigorous, energetic.

(18) **Contented** Easily satisfied with what he has, rarely envious.

**Chief** Commands leadership and expects people to follow.

**Chartmaker** Organizes life, tasks, and problem-solving by making lists, forms, or graphs.

**Cute** Precious, adorable, center of attention.

(19) **Perfectionist** Places high standards on himself and often on others, desiring that everything be in proper order at all times.

**Pleasant** Easygoing, easy to be around, easy to talk with.

**Productive** Must constantly be working or achieving, often finds it very difficult to rest.

**Popular** Life of the party and therefore much desired as a party guest.

(20) **Bouncy** A bubbly, lively personality, full of energy.

**Bold** Fearless, daring, forward, unafraid of risk.

**Behaved** Consistently desires to conduct himself within the realm of what he feels is proper.

**Balanced** Stable, middle-of-the-road personality, not subject to sharp highs or lows.

## Definitions of Weaknesses

(21) **Blank** A person who shows little facial expression or emotion.

**Bashful** Shrinks from getting attention, resulting from self-consciousness.

**Brassy** Showy, flashy, comes on strong, too loud.

**Bossy** Commanding, domineering, sometimes overbearing in adult relationships.

(22) **Undisciplined** A person whose lack of order permeates most every area of his life.

**Unsympathetic** Finds it difficult to relate to the problems or hurts of others.

**Unenthusiastic** Tends to not get excited, often feeling it won't work anyway.

**Unforgiving** One who has difficulty forgiving or forgetting a hurt or injustice, apt to hold on to a grudge.

(23) **Reticent** Struggles against or is unwilling to get involved, especially when such involvement is complex.

**Resentful** Often holds ill feelings as a result of real or imagined offenses.

**Resistant** Strives, works against, or hesitates to accept any other way but his own.

**Repetitious** Retells stories and incidents to entertain you without realizing he has already told the story several times before; is constantly needing something to say.

(24) **Fussy** Insistent over petty matters, calling for a great attention to trivial details.

**Fearful** Often experiences feelings of deep concern, apprehension, or anxiousness.

**Forgetful** Lack of memory, which is usually tied to a lack of discipline and not bothering to mentally record things that aren't "fun."

**Frank** Straightforward, outspoken; doesn't mind telling you exactly what he thinks.

(25) **Impatient** A person who finds it difficult to endure irritation or wait for others.

**Insecure** One who is apprehensive or lacks confidence.

**Indecisive** The person who finds it difficult to make any decision at all (not the personality that labors long over each decision in order to make the perfect one).

**Interrupts** A person who is more of a talker than a listener, who starts speaking without even realizing someone else is already speaking.

(26) **Unpopular** A person whose intensity and demand for perfection can push others away.

**Uninvolved** Has no desire to listen or become interested in clubs, groups, activities, or other people's lives.

**Unpredictable** May be ecstatic one moment and down the next, or willing to help but then disappears, or promises to come but forgets to show up.

**Unaffectionate** Finds it difficult to verbally or physically demonstrate tenderness openly.

(27) **Headstrong** Insists on having his own way.

**Haphazard** Has no consistent way of doing things.

**Hard to Please** A person whose standards are set so high that it is difficult to ever satisfy them.

**Hesitant** Slow to get moving and hard to get involved.

(28) **Plain** A middle-of-the-road personality without highs or lows and showing little, if any, emotion.

**Pessimistic** While hoping for the best, this person generally sees the down side of a situation first.

**Proud** One with great self-esteem who sees himself as always right and the best person for the job.

**Permissive** Allows others (including children) to do as they please so as not to be disliked.

(29) **Angers Easily** One who has a childlike flash-in-the-pan temper that expresses itself in tantrum style and is over and forgotten almost instantly.

**Aimless** Not a goal-setter, with little desire to be one.

**Argumentative** Incites arguments generally because he feels he is right no matter what the situation may be.

**Alienated** Easily feels estranged from others, often because of insecurity or fear that others don't really enjoy his company.

(30) **Naïve** Simple and childlike perspective, lacking sophistication or comprehension of what the deeper levels of life are really about.

**Negative Attitude** One whose attitude is seldom positive and is often able to see only the down or dark side of a situation.

**Nervy** Full of confidence, fortitude, and sheer guts, often in a negative sense.

**Nonchalant** Easygoing, unconcerned, indifferent.

(31) **Worrier** Consistently feels uncertain, troubled, or anxious.

**Withdrawn** A person who pulls back to himself and needs a great deal of alone or isolation time.

**Workaholic** An aggressive goal-setter who must be constantly productive and feels very guilty when resting. Is not driven by a need for perfection or completion but by a need for accomplishment and reward.

**Wants Credit** Thrives on the credit or approval of others. As an entertainer, this person feeds on the applause, laughter, and/or acceptance of an audience.

(32) **Too Sensitive** Overly introspective, and easily offended when misunderstood.

**Tactless** Sometimes expresses himself in a somewhat offensive and inconsiderate way.

**Timid** Shrinks from difficult situations.

**Talkative** An entertaining, compulsive talker who finds it difficult to listen.

(33) **Doubtful** Characterized by uncertainty and lack of confidence that something will ever work out.

**Disorganized** Lack of ability to ever get one's life in order.

**Domineering** Compulsively takes control of situations and/or people, usually telling others what to do.

**Depressed** A person who feels down much of the time.

(34) **Inconsistent** Erratic, contradictory; actions and emotions not based on logic.

**Introvert** A person whose thoughts and interests are directed inward; lives within himself.

**Intolerant** Appears unable to withstand or accept another's attitudes, point of view, or way of doing things.

**Indifferent** A person to whom most things don't matter one way or the other.

(35) **Messy** Living in a state of disorder, unable to find things.

**Moody** Doesn't get very high emotionally, but easily slips into lows, often when feeling unappreciated.

**Mumbles** Will talk quietly under the breath when pushed; doesn't bother to speak clearly.

**Manipulative** Influences or manages shrewdly or deviously for his own advantage; will get his way somehow.

(36) **Slow** Doesn't often act or think quickly—too much of a bother.

**Stubborn** Determined to exert his or her own will, not easily persuaded, obstinate.

**Show-off** Needs to be the center of attention, wants to be watched.

**Skeptical** Disbelieving, questioning motives behind words.

(37) **Loner** Requires a lot of private time and tends to avoid other people.

**Lords Over Others** Doesn't hesitate to let you know that he is right or that he is in control.

**Lazy** Evaluates work or activity in terms of how much energy it will take.

**Loud** A person whose laugh or voice can be heard above others in the room.

(38) **Sluggish** Slow to get started, needs a push to be motivated.

**Suspicious** Tends to suspect or distrust others or ideas.

**Short-tempered** Has a demanding, impatience-based anger and a short fuse. Anger is expressed when others are not moving fast enough or have not completed what they have been asked to do.

**Scatterbrained** Lacks the power of concentration or attention; flighty.

(39) **Revengeful** Knowingly or otherwise holds a grudge and punishes the offender, often by subtly withholding friendship or affection.

**Restless** Likes constant new activity because it isn't fun to do the same things all the time.

**Reluctant** Struggles against getting involved or is unwilling to be involved.

**Rash** May act hastily without thinking things through, generally because of impatience.

(40) **Compromising** Will often relax his position, even when right, in order to avoid conflict.

**Critical** Constantly evaluating and making judgments, frequently thinking or expressing negative reactions.

**Crafty** Shrewd. One who can always find a way to get to his desired end.

**Changeable** Has a childlike, short attention span that needs a lot of change and variety to keep him from getting bored.

# Personality Scoring Sheet

Transfer all your X's to the corresponding words on the Personality Scoring Sheets, and add up your totals. For example, if you checked Animated on the profile, check it on the scoring sheet. (Note: The words are in different orders on the profile and the scoring sheets.)

## Personality Scoring Sheet—Strengths

| | *Popular Sanguine* | *Powerful Choleric* | *Perfect Melancholy* | *Peaceful Phlegmatic* |
|---|---|---|---|---|
| 1. | ☐ Animated | ☐ Adventurous | ☐ Analytical | ☐ Adaptable |
| 2. | ☐ Playful | ☐ Persuasive | ☐ Persistent | ☐ Peaceful |
| 3. | ☐ Sociable | ☐ Strong-willed | ☐ Self-sacrificing | ☐ Submissive |
| 4. | ☐ Convincing | ☐ Competitive | ☐ Considerate | ☐ Controlled |
| 5. | ☐ Refreshing | ☐ Resourceful | ☐ Respectful | ☐ Reserved |
| 6. | ☐ Spirited | ☐ Self-reliant | ☐ Sensitive | ☐ Satisfied |
| 7. | ☐ Promoter | ☐ Positive | ☐ Planner | ☐ Patient |
| 8. | ☐ Spontaneous | ☐ Sure | ☐ Scheduled | ☐ Shy |
| 9. | ☐ Optimistic | ☐ Outspoken | ☐ Orderly | ☐ Obliging |
| 10. | ☐ Funny | ☐ Forceful | ☐ Faithful | ☐ Friendly |
| 11. | ☐ Delightful | ☐ Daring | ☐ Detailed | ☐ Diplomatic |
| 12. | ☐ Cheerful | ☐ Confident | ☐ Cultured | ☐ Consistent |
| 13. | ☐ Inspiring | ☐ Independent | ☐ Idealistic | ☐ Inoffensive |
| 14. | ☐ Demonstrative | ☐ Decisive | ☐ Deep | ☐ Dry Humor |
| 15. | ☐ Mixes Easily | ☐ Mover | ☐ Musical | ☐ Mediator |
| 16. | ☐ Talker | ☐ Tenacious | ☐ Thoughtful | ☐ Tolerant |
| 17. | ☐ Lively | ☐ Leader | ☐ Loyal | ☐ Listener |
| 18. | ☐ Cute | ☐ Chief | ☐ Chartmaker | ☐ Contented |
| 19. | ☐ Popular | ☐ Productive | ☐ Perfectionist | ☐ Pleasant |
| 20. | ☐ Bouncy | ☐ Bold | ☐ Behaved | ☐ Balanced |

**Strengths Totals**

## Personality Scoring Sheet—Weaknesses

| | *Popular Sanguine* | *Powerful Choleric* | *Perfect Melancholy* | *Peaceful Phlegmatic* |
|---|---|---|---|---|
| 21. | ☐ Brassy | ☐ Bossy | ☐ Bashful | ☐ Blank |
| 22. | ☐ Undisciplined | ☐ Unsympathetic | ☐ Unforgiving | ☐ Unenthusiastic |
| 23. | ☐ Repetitious | ☐ Resistant | ☐ Resentful | ☐ Reticent |
| 24. | ☐ Forgetful | ☐ Frank | ☐ Fussy | ☐ Fearful |
| 25. | ☐ Interrupts | ☐ Impatient | ☐ Insecure | ☐ Indecisive |
| 26. | ☐ Unpredictable | ☐ Unaffectionate | ☐ Unpopular | ☐ Uninvolved |
| 27. | ☐ Haphazard | ☐ Headstrong | ☐ Hard to Please | ☐ Hesitant |
| 28. | ☐ Permissive | ☐ Proud | ☐ Pessimistic | ☐ Plain |
| 29. | ☐ Angered Easily | ☐ Argumentative | ☐ Alienated | ☐ Aimless |
| 30. | ☐ Naïve | ☐ Nervy | ☐ Negative Attitude | ☐ Nonchalant |
| 31. | ☐ Wants Credit | ☐ Workaholic | ☐ Withdrawn | ☐ Worrier |
| 32. | ☐ Talkative | ☐ Tactless | ☐ Too Sensitive | ☐ Timid |
| 33. | ☐ Disorganized | ☐ Domineering | ☐ Depressed | ☐ Doubtful |
| 34. | ☐ Inconsistent | ☐ Intolerant | ☐ Introvert | ☐ Indifferent |
| 35. | ☐ Messy | ☐ Manipulative | ☐ Moody | ☐ Mumbles |
| 36. | ☐ Show-off | ☐ Stubborn | ☐ Skeptical | ☐ Slow |
| 37. | ☐ Loud | ☐ Lords Over Others | ☐ Loner | ☐ Lazy |
| 38. | ☐ Scatterbrained | ☐ Short-tempered | ☐ Suspicious | ☐ Sluggish |
| 39. | ☐ Restless | ☐ Rash | ☐ Revengeful | ☐ Reluctant |
| 40. | ☐ Changeable | ☐ Crafty | ☐ Critical | ☐ Compromising |
| **Weaknesses Totals** | 9 | 1 | 7 | 7 |
| **COMBINED TOTALS** | 11 | 1 | 14 | 18 |

Once you've transferred your answers to the scoring sheet, added up your total number of answers in each of the four columns and your totals from both the strengths and weaknesses sections, you'll know your dominant personality type. You'll also know what combination you are. If, for example, your score is 35 in Powerful Choleric strengths and weaknesses, there's really little question. You're almost all Powerful Choleric. But if your score is, for example, 16 in Powerful Choleric, 14 in Perfect Melancholy, and 5 in each of the others, you're a Powerful Choleric with a strong Perfect Melancholy. You'll also know, of course, your least-dominant type.

To help you understand more about your personality type, the following pages offer an overview of each type.

## Popular Sanguines

### "Let's do it the fun way"

**Desire:** to have fun

**Emotional needs:** attention, affection, approval, acceptance

**Key strengths:** ability to talk about anything at any time at any place, bubbling personality, optimism, sense of humor, storytelling ability, enjoyment of people

**Key weaknesses:** disorganized, can't remember details or names, exaggerate, not serious about anything, trust others to do the work, too gullible and naïve

**Get depressed when:** life is no fun and no one seems to love them

**Are afraid of:** being unpopular or bored, having to live by the clock, having to keep a record of money spent

**Like people who:** listen and laugh, praise and approve

**Dislike people who:** criticize, don't respond to their humor, don't think they are cute

**Are valuable in work for:** colorful creativity, optimism, light touch, cheering up others, entertaining

**Could improve if they:** got organized, didn't talk so much, learned to tell time

**As leaders they:** excite, persuade, and inspire others; exude charm and entertain; are forgetful and poor on follow-through

**Tend to marry:** Perfect Melancholies who are sensitive and serious, but whom they quickly tire of having to cheer up and by whom they soon tire of being made to feel inadequate or stupid

**Reaction to stress:** leave the scene, go shopping, find a fun group, create excuses, blame others

**Recognized by their:** constant talking, loud volume, bright eyes

## Powerful Cholerics

### "Let's do it my way"

**Desire:** to have control

**Emotional needs:** sense of obedience, appreciation for accomplishments, credit for ability

**Key strengths:** ability to take charge of anything instantly and to make quick, correct judgments

**Key weaknesses:** too bossy, domineering, autocratic, insensitive, impatient, unwilling to delegate or give credit to others

**Get depressed when:** life is out of control and people won't do things their way

**Are afraid of:** losing control of anything (e.g., losing a job, not being promoted, becoming seriously ill, having a rebellious child or unsupportive mate)

**Like people who:** are supportive and submissive, see things their way, cooperate quickly, let them take credit

**Dislike people who:** are lazy and not interested in working constantly, buck their authority, become independent, aren't loyal

**Are valuable in work because they:** can accomplish more than anyone else in a shorter time; are usually right

**Could improve if they:** allowed others to make decisions, delegated authority, became more patient, didn't expect everyone to produce as they do

**As leaders they have:** a natural feel for being in charge, a quick sense of what will work, a sincere belief in their ability to achieve, a potential to overwhelm less aggressive people

**Tend to marry:** Peaceful Phlegmatics who will quietly obey and not buck their authority, but who never accomplish enough or get excited over their projects

**Reaction to stress:** tighten control, work harder, exercise more, get rid of the offender

**Recognized by their:** fast-moving approach, quick grab for control, self-confidence, restless and overpowering attitude

## Perfect Melancholies

### "Let's do it the right way"

**Desire:** to have it right

**Emotional needs:** sense of stability, space, silence, sensitivity, support

**Key strengths:** ability to organize and set long-range goals, have high standards and ideals, analyze deeply

**Key weaknesses:** easily depressed, spend too much time on preparation, too focused on details, remember negatives, suspicious of others

**Get depressed when:** life is out of order, standards aren't met, and no one seems to care

**Are afraid of:** no one understanding how they really feel, making a mistake, having to compromise standards

**Like people who:** are serious, intellectual, deep, and will carry on a sensible conversation

**Dislike people who:** are lightweights, forgetful, late, disorganized, superficial, prevaricating, and unpredictable

**Are valuable in work for:** sense of detail, love of analysis, follow-through, high standards of performance, compassion for the hurting

**Could improve if they:** didn't take life quite so seriously, didn't insist others be perfectionists

**As leaders they:** organize well, are sensitive to people's feelings, have deep creativity, want quality performance

**Tend to marry:** Popular Sanguines for their outgoing personality and social skills, but whom they soon attempt to quiet and get on a schedule

**Reaction to stress:** withdraw, get lost in a book, become depressed, give up, recount the problems

**Recognized by their:** serious and sensitive nature, well-mannered approach, self-deprecating comments, meticulous and well-groomed looks

## Peaceful Phlegmatics
### "Let's do it the easy way"

**Desire:** to avoid conflict, keep peace

**Emotional needs:** sense of respect, feeling of worth, understanding, emotional support

**Key strengths:** balance, even disposition, dry sense of humor, pleasing personality

**Key weaknesses:** lack of decisiveness, enthusiasm, and energy; a hidden will of iron

**Get depressed when:** life is full of conflict, they have to face a personal confrontation, no one wants to help, the buck stops with them

**Are afraid of:** having to deal with a major personal problem, being left holding the bag, making major changes

**Like people who:** will make decisions for them, will recognize their strengths, will not ignore them, will give them respect

**Dislike people who:** are too pushy, too loud, and expect too much of them

**Are valuable in work because they:** mediate between contentious people, objectively solve problems

**Could improve if they:** set goals and became self-motivated, were willing to do more and move faster than expected, could face their own problems as well as they handle those of others

**As leaders they:** keep calm, cool, and collected; don't make impulsive decisions; are well-liked and inoffensive; won't cause trouble; don't often come up with brilliant new ideas

**Tend to marry:** Powerful Cholerics who are strong and decisive, but by whom they soon tire of being pushed around and looked down upon

**Reaction to stress:** hide from it, watch TV, eat, tune out life

**Recognized by their:** calm approach, relaxed posture (sitting or leaning when possible)

It is important to know your personality. The following sections are divided by personality type. Once you know and understand which personality type is yours, you can read the section or sections that most apply to you. Each section offers insight, suggestions, and stories as to what tools and techniques have proven to be most effective for each personality type in its search for spirituality.

# 5 The Popular Sanguine

*Good people, rejoice and be happy in the Lord. Sing all you whose hearts are right.* Psalm 32:11 NCV

Surrounded by spiritual saints, Marita used to think that she was the only one who struggled. She listened to fellow Christian speakers repeatedly quote sage sayings from the work of Oswald Chambers. Upon hearing the nuggets they shared, Marita longed to be as spiritual as others. While *My Utmost for His Highest* had always seemed incomprehensible to her, the shared snippet encouraged her to try again. After reading a page several times, Marita still had no idea what the text was trying to say. She concluded she was just not that spiritual and put the book away until another Chambers quote prompted her to get it out again. Each time the results were the same.

Someone who Marita viewed as spiritually mature shared that she had read the Bible through every year for over thirty years. No wonder she seemed so spiritually mature. Marita had tried to read the Bible through every year but rarely made it past February. She had used the reading guides they passed out in church, where you check off the little box each day. Several times she started from the beginning but got lost in Leviticus. Then she tried following the popular program of reading some of the Old Testament, some of the New Testament, and a Psalm and a Proverb each day. For her, that seemed too confusing, and she didn't stick with it.

Perhaps writing her prayers was the answer. Many people shared how this technique had been effective for them. They had a prayer notebook and a specified appointment with God. Marita bought the needed notebook and set to work on this new routine. However, her life has no routine, and after a short time this plan had failed, too.

Yet Marita could cite situation after situation where God had directed her life, where she had specifically heard his voice. Could she be spiritual without participating in the popular programs?

## Tools and Techniques

One day Marita discovered the updated version of *My Utmost for His Highest,* which had been revised to reflect today's language. Upon reading this new edition, Marita discovered that her disinterest in Oswald Chambers wasn't a spiritual issue but a generational one. Once she could understand what she was reading, Marita found that she was nearly as much of a fan as her saintly sisters were.

Marita also received a copy of a new Bible—in chronological order, commentary included, and arranged in 365 undated daily readings. She began reading it right away (even though it was not January). The combination of the text's order and the commentary offered all new meaning for her. While Marita's schedule rarely allowed for more than a day or two of sequential reading, the fact that the Bible was not dated kept her from feeling so far behind that she gave up.

Personal study showed Marita that Christ's prayer life was both constant and sporadic, a lot like her own. Christ lived his life in constant communion with his heavenly Father, and also had times of intense, focused prayer when he had a specific need or had the space in his journeys. Although Marita felt she had failed in the scheduled written prayer approach, she talked to God almost constantly—in bed, in the shower, in her car, while doing the dishes, and at the office. As someone once said, "I seldom spend fifteen minutes in prayer, but I rarely go fifteen minutes without praying." Marita often prays in "the garden" or on "the mountain," finding that nature draws her close to God. In times of intense need, she may find herself facedown, crying out to God for extended periods of time. While her prayers do not fit the currently touted type, God still hears them. She still receives answers, and God still speaks to her.

These three differences helped to open her eyes to the various approaches people use in relating to God. Some of her perceived failures were a result of using the wrong tools for her and others were because of wrong technique. When Marita first dared to share her experiences with reading Oswald Chambers and the Bible, members of the audience slid hesitantly next to her and whispered, "I'm one of those." When her facial expression said, *How so?*, they responded with "I could never understand *My Utmost*, either," or "I thought I was not spiritual enough," or "I thought I was the only one who wasn't able to read the Bible through." She was not alone! And neither were they. Because each of us is uniquely different, the way we spend time with God will be personal, designed to meet each individual need, to draw each person into an intimate relationship with God.

For those of us who are the Popular Sanguine-type personality, we have long felt second-class spiritually. Most Popular Sanguines have been frustrated when they were unable to keep up with stringent routines in their spiritual disciplines that others seemed to fulfill with no problems. Janet Simcic told us, "I try so hard to be organized. I am irritated beyond belief by people who promote intense organization. I start praying in my chair after reading my devotional. Then I am distracted by a bird, or a phone call, or a scattered thought. Off I go, mind and body—only to find myself four hours later asking God for forgiveness and quickly begging him to answer this prayer or that." We have long believed that we must follow some prescribed program, and if we do not, God, or at least our friends who are doing everything right, will be mad at us.

Dian Sustek was concerned that something was wrong with her. She went to a Christian therapist about her lack of concentration during prayer and devotional time. She says,

> I am the associate teaching director of Community Bible Studies. While God has given me the discipline to study and prepare for lectures, I always felt guilty because my prayer and devotional time was so poor. I would be praying, and all of a sudden I would be moving furniture or accessories in my mind. About forty-five minutes would pass before I caught on to what was happening, and then I would get all mad at myself because I was supposed to be having my prayer time! I told the counselor all about the distractions; I even told him that once I closed myself in a dark closet so there would be no visual distractions, thinking I would be able to focus better. About two minutes into prayer, I turned on the light and began cleaning the closet out. Then I found an outfit I had forgotten about, which I really loved, and ran out of the closet to try it on! That led to . . . About midmorning, I realized what had happened, and I just broke down and cried out to God for forgiveness. After telling all this to Mike (the therapist), he asked me if I had only one time a day for prayer. "Oh, no," I told him, "actually, I talk to God all day. I take him with me everywhere. I speak to him in the car, in lines at the grocery store and the post office—EVERYWHERE! It is as

though he is my closest friend, and he is always there—loving me."

Then Mike said, "Why don't you just remember that? You are having a prayer time, and he is right there with you. You just need to remember that prayer is a two-way conversation, and you are doing all the talking!"

It has been about three or four years since that happened, and I still get distracted, but I always remember that he is here with me all the time. And I have learned to listen more, because my heart's desire is to hear him throughout the day.

As we did research for this book on the different personality types and how they relate and respond to God in their search for spirituality, we found many things in common among almost all Popular Sanguines. Of course, whenever you make generalizations, there are always exceptions. But we believe that if you are a Popular Sanguine, you can relate to most of the following situations.

Marilyn Hogan from Renton, Washington, says,

It takes some maturity as a Christian (and some understanding of who you are as a Popular Sanguine, made that way and understood by God) to stop trying to be who you are not. I know friends who are Perfect Melancholies, and they have this deep, almost brooding time around Easter as they dwell on what Christ suffered, his pain, and the injustice of it all. I can relate somewhat, but not for such long periods of time. I rejoice in the Resurrection, but I don't dwell on it at a specific time. I tend to think about it through the year as I come across it in the Scriptures, but I can't get "deep" about it like they seem to. For years I felt "less than," until I understood that my faith is not based on the depth of sorrow or anguish or concern I feel, but rather on my trust in the living Christ who dwells in me daily, for all eternity.

Marilyn said it well.

## Early Christian Walk

When we look at the basic strengths and weaknesses of the Popular Sanguine, we can see how they are very much a part of the Popular Sanguine's Christian life—especially the new Christian. Some of their strengths include enthusiasm and expression. They have a changeable disposition, and they like spontaneous activities. On the weakness side, the Popular Sanguine tends to forget obligations and does not follow through, is generally undisciplined and easily distracted. When we combine these traits, the Popular Sanguine tends to be a Christian who gets very excited about inviting Christ into his or her life, who shares Jesus with everyone, but who often loses enthusiasm and gets distracted by the next great cause. The Popular Sanguine new Christian is like the seed that fell on the rocky soil:

> "And some fell on rocky soil where there was little depth of earth; the plants sprang up quickly enough in the shallow soil, but the hot sun soon scorched them and they withered and died, for they had so little root. . . . The shallow, rocky soil represents the heart of a man who hears the message and receives it with real joy, but he doesn't have much depth in his life, and the seeds don't root very deeply, and after a while when trouble comes, or persecution begins because of his beliefs, his enthusiasm fades, and he drops out" (Matt. 13:5–6, 20–21 TLB).

One Popular Sanguine told me, "The depth is not always there; so when seeds are planted into the Popular Sanguine personality, there must be enough Powerful Choleric to pull the roots down into deeper soil for that necessary stability. The Popular Sanguine tends to droop in the heat of the day if toiling becomes too boring."

This was true in Jason's life. He told us,

> At sixteen, I accepted Christ, read the Word daily, and was completely excited. At twenty I took part in a preaching internship. Everyone involved called the experience a "success." After

> returning to Bible college, many things happened in the church and in my life that shattered my plans to be a minister and were destructive in the relationship I had with any organized religious group, i.e., the church. I never lost my faith or trust in God. I tried to remain as faithful to God as I could, but without the support and nurturing of a good pastor and congregation, I found myself living away from God. I used my optimism to convince myself the church was a place where negative-minded people went to find an outlet, and it would better serve me to pursue relationships with "happier" people. In some respects, when it came to certain people, I was correct. But I was missing the whole point. Right now I am back on the "road to the Cross," as a local pastor is helping me to refocus on God. I am learning to participate in a church without putting my faith in that church. I am having to FORCE myself to keep a daily journal. It helps me see how far I am moving forward, and it helps with my writing. I'm twenty-six now and in the midst of the stormiest time of my life (marital problems from my being away from God) and the best time of my life (finding, I believe, a balance between church and real faith in God).

Like Jason, as a new Christian, Sharon Merritt used her Popular Sanguine enthusiasm for God. She tried to win everyone she knew to the Lord.

> In 1976, when I rededicated my life to Christ, I was a Bible-carrying, tract-handing-out person. I used to wear long dresses so I could tuck tracts into my knee-highs. I would hand the tracts out in the hallway as I went about my work. When I think back on it, I must have looked pretty silly. It's amazing I didn't lose my job. Soon I got busy with other social aspects, and the tract thing fizzled away. Even now I tend to get totally engrossed in something, and then after a while I lose interest. I host an online Christian chat room. Many times I think of leaving because I feel bored, but I am learning to stick it out through the boring

times because, like anything else, they, too, shall pass. I have had such wonderful experiences ministering to other people on-line.

Leslie Catron found that she has had to work to keep the original Popular Sanguine excitement over her faith. She says,

> I have personally struggled with the loss of passion and emotion that is part of becoming a Christian. As a Popular Sanguine, emotion/passion are very much a part of the "fun" in life, and when the Christian life settles into routine and intellectual study, these elements are often lost. I guess you could say that this has lead to "distraction" for me. It's kind of "is this all there is?" questioning, and that leads to a distant feeling that God is not around. There was a period of several years in my early thirties that LIFE became larger than life. I found myself questioning my relationship with God. Three small children, a sudden change in career with the third "oops" baby, then staying at home, unable to participate in a lot of ministry because of time, changes in some friendships due to leaving the job market, my husband busy providing for the family . . . no fun! DISTRACTIONS! It took some personal reflection, mentoring from a wise saint in my church, and a change in churches to experience a renewal of that firstborn passion. I now take time to infuse that passion with ever-changing ministry opportunities, time for myself and God, doing fun things like going to the beach or the lake, etc., and being sure that I keep myself around new Christians with passion and people that I can witness to about Christ.

As a new Christian, Ida had a great thirst for God but found that other things became a distraction to her. She says,

> When I first surrendered my life to the Lord, I had an immediate hunger for his Word. I was at a youth retreat and read the entire book of John and half of the Psalms in a few hours. I just couldn't get enough of his Word or time alone with him. But

> then my musical ability got in the way of my relationship with him. Being a new believer, I didn't realize that having a relationship with the Lord was what he really wanted. I thought he wanted me to DO something for him. So I started doing a lot of worship leading and singing, and that really kept me from a deep, intimate relationship right away. I also started looking for relationships with guys (I was eighteen), because I thought that's what God wanted for me. This led to an early marriage that ended in divorce. Again, I kind of missed the point that what the Lord wanted was a relationship between himself and me.

Like Ida, Dianne McClintock's hunger for relationship distracted her from her first zeal for God. She says,

> I was so man-addicted, I didn't think I could survive without one in my life. So when God came into my life, I was really gung-ho, and he began to do a wonderful work in me. He led me to a church where I still am to this day. But even though I started out on fire for the Lord, I was lonely, so I sought out another relationship with a guy. I would go to church, get convicted, but then get distracted by the relationship.

That Popular Sanguine excitement gets us going, but if we are not careful, our weaknesses and lack of follow-through can cause us the same problems Jason, Sharon, Leslie, Ida, and Dianne describe. Evelyn Jimenez says, "As a Popular Sanguine, I have to try harder to stay disciplined and organized. It is easier to leave the harder things on my to-do list for last and do all the fun things first." Hopefully as we mature in Christ, our Christian life puts us in balance. Jennifer Phillips said, "My tendency has been to get caught up in Scripture that tells me God will see me through a problem. Then I'm off and running, assured he will take care of me—without taking the time to delve into his Word to give me the meat that will sustain me and ground me in Christ. It's taken me many years, but now I'm disciplining myself to not only read his Word but to sit at his feet. I'm finding not only is he carrying me but giving me the peace that passeth understanding and using me as a light that reflects a confident, mature Christian woman." Laurie Kehler advises Popular Sanguine new Christians with this thought: "You're excited and HUNGRY for God's Word. And you want to try new things—this church and that church. But remember that you need to be around people who will steer you clear of error."

## View of God

Popular Sanguines who had a healthy relationship with their earthly father tend to view God as a loving, affectionate father: someone who will love them unconditionally, to whom they can always come with their cares, and who will comfort them in their difficult times. When you understand that the emotional needs of the Popular Sanguine are attention, affection, approval, and acceptance, it is easy to see how this personality type would view God as one who fills those needs.

Some Popular Sanguines have found that if their earthly father did not exhibit these loving traits, it is difficult for them to view their heavenly Father as having them—even though they want him to. Laurie Kehler said, "Sometimes I struggle with thinking God is ticked at me for being so lax, or that he's hard to please, like my earthly father (this despite what I know from Scripture)." Along the same lines, Dianne McClintock said, "I really try to view God as a loving and affectionate father, but since my dad was hard on us and expected a lot, I tend to think God is the same. Certain times, however, as I have matured in my walk with him, I do feel God is loving and affectionate."

Many Popular Sanguines, especially those who did not have a solid, healthy relationship with their earthly dad, find that they view God as more of a best friend.

Dolores Feitl, a pastor's wife, says, "If you were 'emotionally estranged' from your parents and looked to your friends, then it is easier to view God as a best friend. That was my situation. So I can relate to God as a best friend. My dad was loving and affectionate but nonverbal; therefore, it took a while for me to relate to God as a Father that I could 'hear.' "

A Perfect Melancholy mom told us,

> I just quizzed my resident Popular Sanguine (my son) and he said you were right on your observations about Popular Sanguines. I was amazed at how readily he answered positively to the question about viewing God as his best friend. I struggle to try to comprehend viewing God as my best friend, but my son views any other response as incomprehensible.

Depending on background, it may take a while for the Popular Sanguine to develop a healthy view of God, like Evelyn Jimenez shares:

> I am a Sanguine, and I never did view God as my best friend. My best friend was someone who was close to me like a girlfriend, someone I could talk with over a cup of coffee. I have always viewed God as a loving, affectionate Father. But recently, because of some hurts in relationships, I have learned to view God more as my best friend than I ever did before. I have learned through the hard knocks in life that he truly NEVER leaves us or forsakes us no matter what may be going on in our lives.

Once they are able to view God as either a loving and affectionate father or a best friend, many Popular Sanguines find that they have a very comfortable and casual relationship with him rather than one of fear or judgment. Barbara Lovett says,

> As a Popular Sanguine, I have always viewed God as a very loving and affectionate Father. Probably I am sometimes more informal than I should be. I remember one time, as I was pre-

paring to take a coffee break, I asked God if he would like to join me. I then proceeded to sit down and converse with him as if he were right there in the room with me (which, by the way, I am sure he was—just not drinking coffee). I remember rambling on and on, and then realizing I was not giving him an opportunity to talk. Typical Popular Sanguine behavior. Finally, stopping, putting tape over my mouth, I was then free to just sit and listen to what he had to say to me. It was one of those highlight times. He had so much to say to me, and all of it was invaluable to my situation at that time.

## Relationship, Not Religion

In talking with Popular Sanguines about their spiritual life, we asked about the importance of their relationship with God. We got several comments like "What else is there?" and "As compared to what?" The Popular Sanguine is such a relationship-focused person that many of the Popular Sanguine Christians we asked couldn't even think of God in any other way—they have a relationship with him! Edie Veenstra told us,

> I focus on relationship. I think that is where it is supposed to be—at least that's where Scripture says it is supposed to be. But the funny thing is that, for me, I am also focusing on relationships with God in the Word when I study and look for practical pointers for my Bible class (I teach). I have just been doing *Experiencing God* on my own. The author—Henry Blackaby—has made an incredible statement: "The Bible is about God. It is not about Abraham. It is not about Moses. It is about God. HIS interaction with His people. HIS development of HIS purposes, plans, and ways on the earth." Well, that was a real eye-opener. Of course! Yet how often have I looked at the Bible as understanding MY part in the relationship first! What foolishness. It is always, and will always be, about GOD first.

However, many people have not been taught about a relationship. They have always thought of God as "religion." Dolores Feitl said, "My entire Christian experience (after I invited Christ as BOTH Savior and Lord) has been based on relationship. Having been a Roman Catholic, I had to 'overcome' and 'replace' religion with relationship!"

Speaker Vickey Banks sees "relationship" as her reason for being a speaker and writer:

> The primary reason I feel compelled to do both is because I long for people to know that there is so much more to the Christian life than going to church and being a good person. I desperately want them to know that there is a dynamic, vibrant, personal, intimate relationship with God to be had. However, I don't merely want them to know about it or wish they had it; I so want them to experience it. Maybe it's the Popular Sanguine part of my personality that doesn't want to miss out on anything, but I simply cannot imagine living without this relationship. It brings purpose and meaning to my busy life. Without it, I fear my life would be like that of a hamster running in place on a wheel—I'd be moving all right (and exhausting myself in the process), but never getting anywhere important. My relationship with God is the anchor in my life—it gives me stability and security. It gives me the confident base I need to branch out and stretch myself. What would I speak on and write about without it? As Winnie the Pooh might say, "It would all be just fluff and stuff!"

Vickey sums it up well by saying, "Relationship is not just important to me, it is life!"

Whatever our personality type, we naturally relate to God accordingly, but rather than use only those natural methods, why not expand and enrich our approach and relationship with God? For example, the Popular Sanguine, who naturally has a varied, active, and friendly relationship with God, would do well to add times of silence, time to be alone. As Henri Nouwen says in his book *Out of Solitude*:

> Somewhere we know that without a lonely place our lives are in danger. Somewhere we know that without silence words lose their meaning, that without listening speaking no longer heals, that without distance closeness cannot cure. Somewhere we know that without a lonely place our actions quickly become empty gestures. The careful balance between silence and words, withdrawal and involvement, distance and closeness, solitude and community forms the basis of the Christian life and should therefore be the subject of our most personal attention.[1]

## Worship

As emotional people, Popular Sanguines are moved closer to God by involving their senses. They are naturally creative and colorful, and they decide by feelings. Knowing that, worship for the Popular Sanguine needs to touch their emotions. Tina Minkkinen told us, "I feel him near more when I am emotionally impacted." For most Popular Sanguines, that "emotional impact" comes from either music or nature. Some Popular Sanguines felt that both were really important to them, and others responded more to one than the other.

Like Marita, Evelyn Jimenez and Vickey Banks shared what music and nature do for them in their search for spirituality. Evelyn says, "Music is exciting and expressive. And nature around us gives me a sense of warm feelings that are personal, with the feeling of home, relationships, family, friends, and God's personal touch of his creation on this earth."

Vickey waxed eloquent as she thought of the impact of music and nature on her spiritual life:

> I am moved by music. I attend a church with over 1,600 people in attendance for worship. However, when I close my eyes during the Praise and Worship music, they are no longer there.

> Somehow I am transported alone into the very presence of God. The lyrics become my prayers and I am so cognizant of him and his holiness that, like Moses, I feel I should remove my shoes!
>
> As for nature, I have never gotten over the beauty of the clouds. Every time I fly in an airplane, I look out the window and think of how amazing God is. He actually balances the clouds! He hung the stars in place and knows them all by name! I look down at the varied terrain of this planet and am overcome at the diversity of it all. Mountains and flatlands, snow-capped peaks and dry desert flora. Lakes and oceans, fields and valleys. It's not just the rocks that cry out his name, but his entire creation! I see it and cannot help but think of how incredible he is.

Not every Popular Sanguine is moved by both music and nature. Many prefer music. In fact, Rose Sweet said, "Music is REAL important . . . nature—not at all for me . . . blah!" Dolores Feitl added, "Music is ESPECIALLY important to me. Nature is second." Ida agreed with Dolores, saying, "Music is extremely important to me. Nature is somewhat important—but I can sure worship God through appreciating his creation."

Sharon Merritt is one who finds music especially important to her spiritual life. She said, "I thoroughly enjoy music and praise. I cannot drive in the car without a music tape playing. The praise part of the service is never long enough. If I am asked to greet people, I get frustrated because I miss most of the worship."

Julie Munos told us that singing praises and thanks to his name really brings her into his presence. She also said that an ideal worship service for her would include "some jamming songs that make everybody dance, some worship songs that make everybody weep, and a spirit of worship that causes everyone to forget about themselves and really focus on God." For most Popular Sanguines, music, nature, or a combination of both touch their emotions and bring them to that place where they can really forget about themselves and focus on God.

## Prayer

Prayer is very important to the Sanguine. As a talker, it is easy to talk to God because you can talk all you want and he will listen. Suzy Ryan says, "I love to talk. He is the only one who I don't have to feel guilty about talking to too much. This is a natural flow from my personality."

The prayers of the Popular Sanguine are seldom the type you might hear from a robed reverend during a formal holiday service. While their prayers may not appear as deep as others, they are sincere and from the heart. Julie Munos said, "I learned to pray from friends who became Christians before me. I was impressed with the way they just 'talked' to God like he was sitting next to them and was a real friend. I know now that he is right there and is my best friend." Peg Hueber said, "I often just snuggle down in my favorite blue chair. I feel as though I am right on God's lap and we are having a wonderful time!"

One of the most consistent comments we received from Popular Sanguines regarding their prayer time is that it is "constant." The Popular Sanguine takes to heart the biblical teaching of 1 Thessalonians 5:17, "Pray without ceasing." Rather than having a scheduled, designated time for prayer, most Popular Sanguines seem to keep up a dialogue with God all day long. They pray in the car, in the shower, in bed, and just about anyplace they go! Vickey Banks says, "True to my Popular Sanguine personality, I pray with great variety. My prayers are long and short, heartfelt and hasty. I may lift them up while I am driving, listening, kneeling, lying down, and even speaking." Evelyn Jimenez says, "I view prayer with God as informal. Talking to him throughout the day much like you would do with a friend. And even though God will hear me out in my prayer time, it is difficult to wait and be quiet." Pam Bianco echoes Evelyn's approach, "I have CONSTANT dialogue with God each day. I have shorter, 'official' prayers, but spend a lot of time talking with God as the day goes on." Evelyn Davison says, "I am a conversational pray-er, talking and listening all day."

## Listening

While the Popular Sanguine has no trouble talking to God, just as in all their relationships, they do have to work at listening. The Bible uses the word "listen" or "hear" more than four hundred times, so it must be important for us. James 1:19a NCV says, "My dear brothers and sisters, always be willing to listen and slow to speak." Listening is not something that comes naturally for us Popular Sanguines, but it is something we can learn and something from which we will benefit greatly. Terri Geary says,

> I talk to God all day long, and I love to do so in the car when I'm driving. I still have the times when I "make time" to be sure to listen to him, but it is something I have to discipline myself to do, because I really do want to hear him talk to me. I've improved a lot over the years, and I sometimes can't stand to miss my quiet time, because I have to know he is with me.

Peg Hueber is learning to listen, too. She says, "Sometimes I take a walk and enjoy his presence as I see the beauty of his creation around me. God is teaching me to 'stand still' before him. I stop walking and try to do nothing but listen so I can hear his still, small voice."

Barbara Lovett shared her struggle to listen with us:

> I guess my problem has always been that I talk too much. That was the first comment on my report card in the first grade: "Barbara is a good student, but Barbara talks too much." How patient God is with me. One time I was in a group that decided that for prayer that day, we would all sit for thirty minutes in complete silence and just listen to God. (It was not a Popular Sanguine who came up with this idea.) As I sat there, I kept start-

ing to tell God what was on my mind. Then I would remember: no, we are supposed to be listening to God. So I would pull back the reins and try again. After about five minutes of quieting my mind, God said, "Barbara, I love you." Wow! that was worth being quiet for, and it motivated me to be quiet again. Again, God said, "Barbara, I love you." Being quiet can be quite rewarding. What I discovered in that thirty minutes was that God's love for me motivated me to be quiet and just listen to him. We can also motivate others by our love. It was quite a lesson for me, as I was dealing with a situation where I wanted someone to do the right thing but was unsure how to motivate the person. God's message to me was to love that person for now; love alone will motivate.

For most of us Popular Sanguines, listening is something we have to work at. However, sometimes we don't even want to listen! As Dianne McClintock shared, we know what we should do, and we avoid listening to God because we don't want to hear it! "I always talk to God, all day long, very informally. I know I should listen, but sometimes I don't want to hear what I know he wants to say to me. I think I know what he wants to say already. If he is convicting me about something, I will often turn his voice off."

## Focus and Frustration

Most Popular Sanguines have more of an informal relationship with God. However, some have learned to discipline themselves to a regular daily prayer/study time. While compared to the discipline of the Perfect Melancholy, the Popular Sanguine's daily quiet time may not seem all that "regular," but for the Popular Sanguine it is! Suzy Ryan stated that for her a daily time with God is a must. "Sometimes it is deep and meaningful, but sometimes it is on the run." Vickey Banks, who refers to herself in her note to us as "the Seemingly Sappy Sanguine," says that she often resorts to a weekly prayer cycle to ensure that she prays for everything she needs to. On Monday she prays for the ministry to the Nearly/Newlywed Sunday school class and weekly women's Bible study. On Tuesday, "two plus two—as in my husband and I plus our two children." Wednesday is for workers and world leaders. Thursday Vickey devotes to thanksgiving and Friday is for family and friends. Vickey says, "I am acutely aware that unless I write someone's request down and follow this formula, their needs may fly right out of my brain. Although my intentions are sincere, my follow-through can pale in comparison. I fight this aspect of my personality."

As Vickey shared, her lack of focus is something she fights all the time, something she has had to work on. This is common to almost all Popular Sanguines. Their lack of discipline and lack of focus are frustrating. Janet Simcic says, "We Popular Sanguines are continually frustrated because we compare ourselves to the disciplined Powerful Cholerics and the Perfect Melancholy people in our life—who tend to make us look bad. My only hope is that God was able to use Peter. So there is definitely hope for me. However, all of my 'serious and disciplined' friends always call me when they want to laugh and have some fun!" Leslie Catron told us, "My time with God is important in my mind and is done easily on the run, but I do struggle with 'quiet' time and the discipline of daily prayer. Study time is easy for me as it involves finding new information, helps, and wisdom."

## Guilt and Grace

Popular Sanguines tend to rededicate their life to the Lord at meetings where they are emotionally impacted. Marion Grace Bower from New Zealand offered these comments:

> As a child, I used to go to camp and always recommitted myself to regular prayer and Bible reading, but found that it only lasted a little while. I beat myself up and felt a failure for years, so now I, too, encourage people to just start again and do it as you can. It is not for lack of purpose, but it takes a greater effort

for a Popular Sanguine to maintain regular practices.

As Marion expressed about her own life, many Popular Sanguines feel their need for constant rededication is a sign that they are failing God or that they are not good enough Christians. Terri Geary said, "I used to rededicate myself a lot to the Lord at meetings that were emotionally stimulating—I've grown past the part that is not healthy, but sometimes I am still stuck in beating myself up for being a failure, and I'm still tempted to think God's love is conditional—at times."

Like Terri, some Popular Sanguines struggle with their failures. But most know God loves them anyway and do not get into too much of a bind over it. Linda Shepherd told us, "I don't think spiritual failure keeps Popular Sanguines from trying again. For each day is a new, fresh day." We have found that the Popular Sanguine readily accepts the idea of "grace," having very little trouble with the fact that God will forgive them and that they can start anew. Popular Sanguines do not like to carry lots of guilt. They readily accept the gift of grace as found in Romans 11:6 NCV: "And if he chose them by grace, it is not for the things they have done. If they could be made God's people by what they did, God's gift of grace would not really be a gift." Lory Garrett describes it this way:

> About failing God and guilt, perhaps we Popular Sanguines take God and his grace at face value. We all know salvation can't be earned, it's a gift from God. So condemning ourselves for not earning something that can't be earned anyway is rather silly, and a waste of time. Why not just get on with the life he calls us to? I take heart in what Paul says in 2 Corinthians 12:9 NCV: " 'My grace is enough for you. When you are weak, my power is made perfect in you.' So I am very happy to brag about my weaknesses. Then Christ's power can live in me."

While she did not use the word grace in her explanation to us, Armené Humber offered a beautiful description of her failures and God's release from her guilt:

God relieved me of my guilt one day when I was frustrated with all my failed good intentions. I just couldn't keep the devotional schedule that I kept making for myself. It was sort of like a perpetual New Year's resolution that lasted twenty-four hours. I would commit to an early morning time and then find a million things that needed doing in the early morning. I tried an evening time and promptly fell asleep after about ten verses. I remember one day doing dishes and beating myself up about all of this. What was wrong with me? Didn't I care about Jesus? Was I just lazy? I couldn't stick with it. I probably would have fallen asleep in the Garden of Gethsemane and missed the whole crucifixion! Jesus couldn't count on me. Then, in the middle of this whole self-torture session, I felt like God said to me, in a voice that a father would use to distract a miserable child, "I tell you what. Let's do this. . . . You go ahead and get busy with your day. But keep your ears open and listen for my voice. I will pick a time and place to meet you, and when it is ready I will call you. It will be a surprise each day. When you hear me call, you meet me, and we will have our special time together." It was suddenly like a game. Never the same place, never the same time. Anyway, the point is that in doing that, God took all the "shoulds" out of my meeting with him and instead of "having devotions," I had intimacy, and I developed a sharpened ear that got used to listening for his voice. This helped me to learn that God accepted me just as I am and taught me that I can count on him to even design the disciplines of spiritual growth around who he had made me to be. He is so good!

Isn't intimacy with God what it is all about?

## Study Time

As we talked with, interviewed, and received surveys from Popular Sanguines all over the world, we found that those who do have a study time have one that is true to the Popular Sanguine personality. Their study time is varied, often trying the newest book or latest trend. Evelyn Jimenez affirmed this observation as she said, "It is sometimes difficult to finish a certain book I am reading without stopping and wanting to go on to the next thing. Or even reading two books at the same time and finding that it is easy to put them down and feel perfectly OK if you did not finish reading them because something more interesting came along." (We do hope that you are able to finish this book, at least the section that pertains to your personality!) Leslie Catron adds, "Don't leave out that we really like Christian novels." This is certainly true in Marita's life. She belongs to a Christian inspirational book club through which she receives four Christian novels a month. She usually reads them all. Through the medium of fiction, especially Christian fiction, valuable truths are taught in an easy-to-assimilate fashion. These inspirational Christian novels are an excellent way to teach a young Popular Sanguine woman (or teen) about God.

## Journalizing

Journalizing is not something that is attractive to all Popular Sanguines, though many do feel that it is helpful and they should try to do it more often. The general observation is that the Popular Sanguine journals sporadically, if at all. Marilyn Hogan said, "Journalizing? I have had that laid on me for years . . . and I tried, and tried, and then said to myself: 'Do I really want someone reading my innermost thoughts after I am dead and gone?' " Hmmm, I hadn't thought of that! Janet Simcic faced a typical Popular Sanguine problem with journalizing. She said, "I tried writing my prayers, like Fred Littauer suggested. But I kept losing my notebook."

Many Popular Sanguines do try to journal. They may hear a speaker talk about its benefits and go home with that renewed commitment, which is so typical of the Popular Sanguine's personality—

to try again. Dianne McClintock found that to be true in her life. She kept trying. She told us, "If too much time has gone by, I start a new one because I don't want to be inconsistent in dates. For example: the first entry is 1/2/97, the second is 1/5/97 (that's okay), but the third is 5/25/97? No way, gotta start a new journal." Evelyn Jimenez adds, "And then when you do journal, it has to be a beautiful, colorful journal. Not a dull, unexciting notebook. And if after you get started you lose the journal, you lose interest in proceeding. I have several journals I began but never finished."

As we can see, the Popular Sanguine who does journal tends to do it in spurts—often when they are going through something they need to process or when God is really working in their lives. Shauna Skye told us, "When I learn a spiritual truth, or if something clicks for me, my first impulse is to write it down." Likewise, Sue Foster says, "I do not journal as often as I would like. When God is opening up a new truth to me, I journal like crazy and write pages."

Armené Humber recalls,

> I had forgotten that the reason I began journaling was because I was so discouraged about the legalistic teaching—the shoulds—that were suffocating me so badly. My very first entry came three years after I was a Christian and was just a cry for God to take me back to the place where I could come to him "just as I am." I was frustrated that "just as I am" was okay for salvation but not for how I related to him from then on. My journals are sprinkled with my quest to learn who I am and to rediscover God's acceptance of me, which had been so sweet at salvation.

Marita has a unique form of journalizing—she does it via e-mail! It usually happens when a close friend who knows that she is facing some difficulties sends her an e-mail asking how things are. As Marita sits down at the computer to respond to the question, her fingers fly across the keyboard—originally full of typos! Before long she discovers she has written as many as five single-spaced pages! Pouring out her thoughts and feelings is a catharsis for her. Once she has taken the time to write all that out, she sends it to not only the friend who asked about it, but to all of her good personal buddies on her e-mail list. The computer saves the file automatically, so she has a record of her thoughts and growth, and her friends are kept up-to-date on her life. Only a Popular Sanguine would send her journals out over the Internet!

Some Popular Sanguines use their journal to process feelings, to record growth, or to connect with God. Armené Humber says,

> I began journalizing a long, long time ago, and it is really a special thing in my life. But God has used my pen and seems to connect with me the minute I put it to paper. I do not make myself journal. I journal when I feel like it, often going months without journalizing a thing. I usually just write one page unless I am "unloading." My format is a letter to God. I start "Dear God," or "Precious Abba." I pour my heart out to him, and find that about halfway through the page, he is answering me with Scripture, encouragement, challenge, new thoughts, etc. These journals have become the basis for my devotional writing and the ideas for other types of writing. They are my record of spiritual growth, but they are not "must do's." One of the great things about Popular Sanguines' search for spirituality is the freedom they feel in their relationship with God.

As Armené says, it is not the "shoulds" or the "must do's," but more the relationship and intimacy.

## Trauma or Crisis

Many Popular Sanguines who have overcome their natural tendencies toward inconsistency, lack of discipline, and boredom have done so because of trauma or crisis in their life. Those difficult times bring Popular Sanguines closer to God. Edie Veenstra says,

> Crisis and trauma did bring me closer to the Father. It is something that continually impacts me. Because as much as I think I am all-together, I realize that only the heavenly Father has the answer. I know he wants it to work out. But this is where the relationship with him is so exciting. There are always many ways a problem can be solved. And he has brought about the most creative ways to solve my problems. He is wonderful.

Ida Rose Heckard confirms Edie's thoughts: "Trauma has definitely brought me closer to God. Infertility, losing my mother-in-law to breast cancer, having twins, surviving ovarian cancer, going through a church split, unemployment—all these have brought me MUCH closer to the Lord." Sharon Merritt said, "When I was going through the illness and death of my daughter, I found I was forced to evaluate my relationship with the Lord and either give it up or draw closer to him. I found my faith became stronger than ever." And Sue Foster told us, "I have found that a crisis always brings me closer to God and reveals a new lesson through it. However, this past year I feel close to God always and do not need a crisis to turn to him. It's a wonderful way to live."

Judy Hampton told us about a serious difficulty in her life involving her son's substance abuse, financial difficulties, job changes, and estrangement. She said that the heartache was more than she could bear. At that time a friend came to her and asked her, "Judy, how much time do you spend in prayer?" Judy says,

> I was embarrassed to admit that my feelings were running my life, which in turn kept me from spending much time at all in prayer, reading God's Word, or trusting him for anything. My dear friend pointed out that my state of mind and emotions were the obvious result of prayerlessness. I thought about her wise remarks for a few days and soon became convicted. I knew I needed to make some serious changes in my life. First I went to the Lord and asked him to forgive me for trying to run my life apart from

> him. Then I began gathering materials to begin organizing my prayer life. I developed a prayer journal, which broke prayer down into various sections, and began pursuing a consistent, strong prayer life. Because I made a commitment to the Lord to spend time with him, my priorities had to change. I knew I had to have my prayer time first thing every morning, or it would never take place. I began using several devotionals for my worship and Bible study. Books like *My Utmost for His Highest* or *Streams in the Desert*. When the Spirit of God spoke to me through his Word, I would write it down in my journal. What comfort the living Word brought. I made a decision to list all my sins on paper. What a relief to ask God for his unconditional forgiveness. One of those sins was a rebellious spirit, thinking I didn't need a prayer life! I began confessing my sin of worry and anxiety. Finally I began to pray about everything and to thank God for everything (Phil. 4:6). I was even able to thank him for our prodigal son.
>
> The results were almost immediate! Our situation hadn't changed, but I was changing. I became a truth-seeker, not a rights-defender. God began to fill me with his peace that passes all understanding. I reached a point where I could honestly say, "Lord if I never see our son again, I know you are sufficient for all things, and that you are in control. I choose to trust your Word that says you will supply all my needs according to your riches in Jesus Christ." I was being transformed.

Ultimately, Judy's son's life was straightened out, by giving his life to Jesus. But that time of severe heartache began a daily time of prayer, worship, and study, which she has maintained ever since!

Armené said,

> It was during my life crisis just eight years ago that I finally found what worked for me. Up until then it had been a hit-and-miss sort of thing. Like Marita, I discovered the chronological

*Daily Bible* (published by Harvest House), and it was like going to my mailbox every day to get my mail from God to ME! I made a devotional basket that I could carry with me to any chair, and it made it easier to have everything I needed to communicate with God. Along with my chronological Bible, I kept my *NIV Study Bible*, some notepads, a devotional book or two, and a pencil case with a highlighter. Of course my journal was always there. And my routine, once I defined it, was a source of security for me. I would get up at 5:30, take my cup of Swiss mocha and sit in my recliner, wrap up in an afghan, and open my "mail." It seemed that there was something for each day that I would be facing. It was an incredible time. I have since added pretty file folders so that I can slip notes into them and write on topics that I seem to be getting a lot of stuff on. I now keep writing pads, too, because God is giving me insights that I know I must write down.

## Popular Sanguine to Popular Sanguine

If you are a Popular Sanguine, rejoice in who he made you to be. Laura Riley offers encouragement to all Popular Sanguines through her story:

I have been a Christian most of my adult life but have always struggled with developing an intimate relationship with God; that is, until I understood the unique design in which God fashioned me—a Popular Sanguine! Prior to being introduced to this concept, I viewed God as simply a serious, no-nonsense type father, who surely didn't have time for laughter or friendship. I failed to see how building a relationship with him could be fun, and since I love to have fun, my prayer life and commitment to daily Bible study were hit-and-miss. Structure does not come naturally to me, and I figured if I didn't have time with God at the same time every day, in the same way, I was somehow failing him. I viewed quiet times as more punishment than privilege.

Once I discovered my personality and uncovered that God created me a Popular Sanguine, it was like a cork popped off a bulging bottle. What release I felt! I realized that since he made me, he knows me better than anyone. He knows I like to laugh and have fun. He knows I thrive on activity and the attention of others. He also knows I am easily distracted and that a daily constant requires great discipline for me. But once I understood these things about myself and could accept them, it gave me a greater understanding of the God who created me. I suddenly viewed him as my friend as well as my Father. My prayer life and personal relationship with him have blossomed dramatically since the day I met the Popular Sanguine inside of me. I now enjoy spending time with God and take absolutely everything to him in prayer. I am constantly amazed at how quickly he seems to answer my prayers now, too. Perhaps it is because before understanding who I am in Christ, I prayed with anxiety; now I pray with expectancy!

He gives me undivided attention for as long as I want—every Popular Sanguine's dream! I no longer try to cram myself into a mold that doesn't fit—like having a quiet time every day at 6:00 A.M.! I spend time with him daily—but the time of day differs. I used to think I had to speak in fancy rhetoric and follow a specific formula when praying; and I never got a darn thing out of it! Now I simply talk to God like I talk to any of my friends—I pour out my feelings, share my thoughts, pose my questions, and wait for his answers. Some of my best talks with God have been at midnight, in my pajamas, curled up on the couch with a cup of hot chocolate. My relationship with God is now my first priority—he truly is my best friend. I am so thankful he made me a Popular Sanguine, because I love getting to know him!

We have found that many Popular Sanguines have felt like Laura. We encourage you to discover who God made you to be and to connect with him on that level or in that capacity. Fellow Popular Sanguines offer some help in your search for spirituality that fits who you are. Sue Foster advises, "I firmly believe that God loves us no matter what, and he loves any time we spend with him. I would encourage other Popular Sanguines not to give up. It boils down to what is the most important thing to you. But don't feel guilty just because you don't spend the hours that a Melancholy or Phlegmatic would."

Our "Seemingly Sappy Sanguine" friend Vickey Banks suggests,

> Being in a small group Bible study made a significant difference in my relationship with God. I learned how to have a meaningful quiet time and was required to memorize Scripture. I was taught about God and prayed for. Completing the lessons required personal discipline and time management. It made me hungrier to know God and his Word. Valuable? Immeasurably so. Would I recommend it? I'd require it if I could.

Like Vickey, Marion Bower found that not only was involvement in a group study helpful but organizing and teaching one forced her to stay focused. She says,

> A very successful time was when we ran a family home group while I was in Tasmania. We started with a potluck dinner so the adults and children had time to socialize over the meal. We took our own plates and utensils, and when we were finished we put them all in our bag and took them home so we didn't waste time on chores. The children had their time with an adult who worked specifically with them. That way the adult group was able to get straight down to study with no distractions. This was perfect for everyone, but especially for the Popular Sanguines who love a party and talking time and are then able to settle down to focus on Bible Study and prayer with an 'empty cup' (we had emptied out all the daily routine and cares before we came together so there was an ability to go straight to the heart of the matter and use our relationship, sense of belonging, and fun to enhance our time together).

As a Popular Sanguine, Suzanne Lepkowski has found what works for her family: "I think the key for this sanguine family is PARTICIPATION! If we can't participate, it isn't fun, and for a sanguine it is not worth doing or won't get done as frequently."

Overall, the advice Popular Sanguines offer to other Popular Sanguines who are searching for spirituality is: Do not worry about guilt, just get started, even if it is only five minutes a day. Be in a study group to help stay disciplined and focused.

## A Reminder to Other Personality Types

Throughout this section we have been encouraging Popular Sanguines in their search for spirituality. We hope that they have seen that God made them the way they are and they are not alone in their feelings of failure or shortcoming. We hope they have been encouraged, affirmed, and challenged into an intimate relationship with God that is natural for the Popular Sanguine.

However, if you have been reading this section and are not a Popular Sanguine, we hope that you have seen the ways Popular Sanguines approach God and how their attitude might be different from yours but still be OK. This is important for you to understand, lest your good intentions attempt to force a Popular Sanguine into a mold that does not fit her—thus causing her to fall away from her faith. The following story shared with us by Sue Roberts illustrates why understanding and accepting the various paths to spirituality are so imperative within our churches and families.

> I was raised Catholic, which, in my experience, is a very Melancholy church—not much FUN. We also raised our three sons Catholic, and the one who was sanguine, at age seventeen said, "Enough" and left for a big megachurch in town that had great music, trips, parties, etc. After joining the church and getting rebaptized, he joined the choir because they had a great trip to the

> Holy Land coming up—even though he never sang a single note (they did require him to move his mouth, but he didn't have to sing). He saved money for a whole year, went to the Holy Land for Christmas Day, and sang (lip-synched) in Manger Square on Christmas morning. During the Easter season he participated in their very professional Easter production and was cast as one of the twelve disciples. He was also part of the video team. Shortly after that some of the older members of the church took a disliking to him, partly because of his Popular Sanguine traits of being loud without much follow-through and also for not growing spiritually in the way they believed he should have. As a result, he walked out of the church altogether and hasn't gone near a church in years. It's very sad to all of us, but I have been thankful for my knowledge of the personalities, because it is a tremendous help in understanding what went wrong.

We need to be aware of the personalities of others and encourage them to grow and develop as God made them, not to fit some preconceived idea of what a spiritual person should look, act, or sound like. While we all may be different, we can all have a heart for God.

Marilyn Hogan offers encouragement to all Popular Sanguines in their search for spirituality. She says, "I think it will be encouraging to many that they are not lone rangers out there—alone with these characteristics—and they are not 'less than' as believers, either."

And to the more serious personalities, our Popular Sanguine advice is from Psalm 51:12: "Restore to me again the joy of your salvation." Lighten up! Glorify God and enjoy him forever!

# The Powerful Choleric

# 6

*But by the grace of God I am what I am, and his grace to me was not without effect. No, I worked harder than all of them—yet not I, but the grace of God that was with me.* 1 Corinthians 15:10

## God . . . Do Something! Now! Here, Let Me Help!

With each personality type, our natural traits are expressed in our relationship with God. When we review the characteristics of Powerful Cholerics as found in chapter 4, we see that they are independent and self-sufficient, exude confidence, and can run anything. Coupled with these strengths are weaknesses such as: they know everything, can do everything better, and are too independent. Add these up, and you can easily see why "control" is one of the major traits of Powerful Cholerics.

Some of the other strengths that manifest themselves repeatedly in Powerful Cholerics' search for spirituality are that they are born leaders, dynamic and active, and have a need to correct wrongs. Some of the companion weaknesses are: they believe the end justifies the means and they can't relax. This combination of traits makes the spiritual side of Powerful Cholerics very action-oriented.

Additionally, Powerful Cholerics are known as people who are goal-oriented. They organize well and see the whole picture. As a result, "goals" are very important to Powerful Cholerics in their search for spirituality. When thinking of Powerful Cholerics and their spiritual life, remember three key words: *control*, *action*, and *goals*.

Popular author Patsy Clairmont agrees. She told us, "Control, action, and goals—right on, sisters! I say a rousing YES to each of those definitions as I consider my driving forces. And when I am not skipping through life's garden paths (my Popular Sanguine), I'm hotfooting it down life's freeways, leaving occasional skid marks as I screech past the slow folks."

## Control

The fact that God is sovereign causes major problems for the Powerful Choleric. Sovereignty tells us that God is in control of all things. But most Powerful Cholerics want to be in control themselves. We tend to think he's not doing as fine or as fast a job as we could. Because of Betty's impatience, if change doesn't happen quickly—if God is not fast enough, she is likely to step in and retake the problem into her own hands. She would like to believe that it is because of her tenacity, hard work, and self-control that her family will turn out well. Add to that tendency the inherent responsibility mothers feel toward their daughters, and you can begin to understand why Betty had such a struggle letting go of Kristi and entrusting her to the Lord (as discussed in chapter 1). She has found that the main areas of her life in which the Lord is constantly working are control, patience, and trust. Like most Powerful Cholerics, Betty's motto in life might well be, "Don't just stand there, do something. Now!"

Speaking of her Powerful Choleric husband, Judy said, "The world revolves around his leading at his job and at home. Letting go and letting God was a hard concept for him to grasp. 'Let go' is not in a Powerful Choleric's vocabulary or makeup." Jason Wrench had an interesting experience that taught him, as a Powerful Choleric, to learn to trust Jesus and put aside his own control issues. It happened when he was in high school and his parents signed him up to go on a Christian retreat. He said,

> I wasn't too keen on the idea, since I really didn't know too much about the organization, but I reluctantly agreed to go—on the condition that I could leave the place at any time if I decided that it just wasn't for me.
>
> I was to arrive at the retreat facility on a Wednesday morning. I got there and immediately put up all of my defenses. For the first time in my entire life, I was left with a complete group of strangers. I felt so completely out of control. After everyone was inside the building, the first thing the retreat leaders did was take away our watches. Some people don't understand why I had this obsessive compulsion with losing my watch, but I did. To me, my watch represented everything about my life that was stable and organized. I felt that I could handle almost anything if I could just see how long I would have to endure it. After reluctantly placing my watch in a paper sack and writing my name on it in big, BOLD letters, I gave it to the retreat leader almost with a tear in my eye.
>
> After our first session, I went back to my room and found a hand-crafted yarn wristband with the note, "I know that you've lost your watch; instead wear this stylish swatch!" It was brightly colored and had a big sticker on it where the watch face should

> have been, with the words TRUST JESUS!
>
> Throughout the course of the weekend, I learned that I could put all of my control-oriented issues aside and truly lean on Jesus. I had to trust the people who were leading the retreat to get me to where I needed to be at all times. I also had to learn to trust Jesus with a lot of other issues in my life. Who would have known that a simple act like placing my watch aside for an entire weekend could have changed my life, but it did!

Many Powerful Cholerics do not give God control of their lives until they have tried to do it on their own and failed. Dianne McClintock told us what she learned when her own efforts didn't work:

> I had a true opportunity to see God at work in my life when I was at the end of my rope in relationships with men. I had gone from one guy to the next, always trying to fix him and make him the guy God would approve of for me. Of course, it never worked, and I had a particularly horrible ending of the relationship with my last boyfriend. I was struck with the fact that I was attracting basically the same kind of man again and again. I was going to church and trying to draw close to God while living in sin between services.
>
> After the last episode, I finally threw my hands in the air, and with absolute admission of my sin and desire for God's will in my life, I asked God to never allow another man to come into my life unless he was the one God had designed for me. Within one month he showed me who my husband was to be—he was someone I had known at church for almost a year, and I wasn't even attracted to him. We have been married for five years, and I have to say it has been the best five years of my life and continues to be better and better every day. My husband is being groomed for an associate pastoral position at our church. (Quite a long way from the deadbeat guys I used to go after!)

While it is not easy, the Powerful Choleric can give control to

God; it is something that we can learn. However, like Isabelle Bishop and Kathie Butler, most Powerful Cholerics find that it is a continual process. Isabelle said,

> I am a strong Powerful Choleric. I am in control of most of my life. Recently I had to give God control of an important area of my life. It has been the hardest thing I have ever had to do. My oldest daughter (Elisabeth, fourteen) is from my first marriage. She has been going to her dad's house every other week since she was very small. I now have two small children from my second marriage. The children are not what Elisabeth expected them to be. She doesn't get all the attention anymore, and she is no longer happy at my house. This Mother's Day she told me that she wanted to live at her dad's house on a permanent basis. I was distraught. I have been told I can fight it, but I don't think it is worth it—emotionally or financially. So I have had to let go of Elisabeth—give her to God and trust that all the values I have taught her will guide her through her teenage years. I want to take back the control. I give her to God, and then I worry. I try to analyze and plan to make it right. I can't do that. I really have to give up complete control and trust in God that she will still love me and she will come out OK. It is like King Solomon. He had two women fighting over one child. Instead of seeing the child cut in half, the real mom gave her child up. That is exactly how I feel. My child was split in half for way too long. I just hope the end result will be that she will see that I really love her. It has been hard to give up my child—and to give up control.

Kathie Butler told us,

> There have been many times in my life that I have professed that I have given every aspect of my life to God, only to turn around the very next day and take every bit of it back. It is a major roller coaster. My biggest thing to give up and take back is the relationship portion of my life. I have had millions of dis-

cussions with God, asking him why I can't have the kind of relationship that so-and-so has or why I can't be happily married with kids of my own? I must be some sort of a "disaster magnet." It seems that every relationship I have been involved in turns out to be a major disaster, primarily because I try to take control. I have been married twice, and both marriages ended in divorce. I have dated several people for many years, but I never seem to find one that will make a "total" commitment to me.

Recently I've had a real hard time with my biological clock. I just turned thirty-eight, and I am not in a relationship at this time, nor are there any prospects. I never thought that I wanted to be a mom, but lately (since I turned thirty-six) I have had a desperate urge to have a child. The weekend of my birthday, I got two separate phone calls, both from my sisters-in-law (I am older than either of them), stating that they were pregnant and delivering within a few months of each other.

Although I am very excited for each of them and very happy that I get to be an aunt, I couldn't help but hold a pity party for myself. I was in this deep, dark funk, and was totally inconsolable. Several of my friends that are in a support group with me tried to help, but it was a disaster, and no one was able to get me out of this mood. Finally my dear Perfect Melancholy friend reminded me that this was the one part of my life that I supposedly gave to God about two years ago, after a failed relationship, and I was not letting God take care of it. About once a week she has to remind me that God will find the right guy at the right time for me. She had me do this little exercise: I close my eyes and pretend I'm standing at the bottom of a stairway with a box in my hands. I'm supposed to imagine the thing that I'm giving to God is in that box, and that God is waiting at the top of the stairs. I climb the stairs, hand the box to God, and turn around to descend the stairs. I'm allowed to look back to see that God has opened my box and has already begun to take care of my concern (whatever it is). That seems to satisfy me. Being a Powerful

Choleric, I like to see things being taken care of and to know that I put it into play.

Kathie's exercise would be a valuable one to implement for all Powerful Cholerics who struggle with control.

A good verse to memorize, or place on the mirror in the bathroom or on the dashboard of the car, is 1 Chronicles 29:11: "Yours is the mighty power and glory and victory and majesty. Everything in the heavens and earth is yours, O Lord, and this is your kingdom. We adore you as being in control of everything."

## Action

While the Popular Sanguine easily accepts the concept of grace, the Powerful Choleric is drawn to the idea of justification. The latter believes that while good works are not the grounds for our salvation, they are the certain consequence of justification (Rom. 6:14; 7:6). Many Powerful Cholerics claim James 2:20–26 as their mantra. It says, "You foolish man, do you want evidence that faith without deeds is useless? . . . You see that a person is justified by what he does and not by faith alone. . . . As the body without the spirit is dead, so faith without deeds is dead." Most of the people you find in pro-life marches or picketing abortion clinics are either Powerful Cholerics themselves or those stirred to action by the motivating words of a Powerful Choleric. These people feel they are called to stand up for righteousness and for social responsibility.

## Works

Marita once had such an employee. She held strong anti-abortion convictions. She pushed the speakers represented by CLASServices whose speech topics reflected social concerns. She was incensed when Marita would not redo the company materials to include a pro-life statement on every piece of literature that went out of the office.

While CLASServices is not an organization dedicated to social concerns, there are many Christian organizations whose mission is action. They exist to bring about change and to call people to address social concerns. Focus on the Family has become one such organization, although it did not start out that way. A *U.S. News and World Report* cover story on Dr. James Dobson said that "Focus . . . is also the center of a pro-family culture that is a kind of parallel universe to mainstream popular culture." In that same article, Dr. Dobson is clearly described as both a man of action and a Powerful Choleric. Although the term Powerful Choleric is not used, it is noted how closely the comments reflect the traits of the Powerful Choleric. The article quotes one former employee who says of Dobson, "He believes strongly in his rightness." This is true of most Powerful Cholerics. In order to embrace a cause fully, they must believe they are right, and this is something that comes naturally to the Powerful Choleric.

When asked about his stand, Dobson says,

> I care deeply about the moral tone of the nation. I care about right and wrong. I have deep convictions about absolute truth. . . . I will fight that evil as long as there is breath within my body. . . . I guess it irritates me when people who know what is right put self-preservation and power ahead of moral principle. That is more offensive to me, in some ways, than what Bill Clinton does with interns at the White House. . . . It is never wrong to do what's right. And you stand for what is right whether it is strategic or not.[1]

When we string the quotes together, you can see a profile of a man with great convictions, a man who will stand up for what he believes in—he is a Powerful Choleric!

Jody Antrim told us she has found the best way to get a Powerful Choleric into church is through participation in a cause: "One of the largest areas in which I have seen Cholerics come to know God is through Habitat for Humanity. Building a home is a concrete way for Cholerics to serve God."

While being active is an admirable trait, Gary Thomas offers the following advice:

> Activists need to learn the message of Habakkuk 2:4—living by faith. Life situations and circumstances can tempt us to question God's sovereignty and goodness, but we see with a finite eye. God is not blind to injustice, nor is he indifferent.
>
> The activist must be careful that intercession doesn't become accusation. Because there is so much apathy in the world—even in the church—it is very easy for an activist to feel isolated and alone. We see the injustice, we see wickedness passed off as good, and our hearts burn within us, yet when we look around, the church seems to be sleeping. This can create an isolation that, if not kept in perspective, can eventually be broadened to include "apathy" of God. Not only will the church not respond, the activist thinks, but even God is silent. When we think our concern for righteousness exceeds God's, we have slipped into the delusion of being self-appointed messiahs. "Behold the proud, his soul is not upright in him; but the just shall live by faith."[2]

Social responsibility, or "works," is just one of the ways the trait of action is evident in the life of the Powerful Choleric. Other aspects of the Powerful Choleric's search for spirituality also reflect the need for action.

## Goals

Goals are a natural part of the Powerful Choleric's personality. As Jeff Russell expressed,

> Goals are necessary because they form the foundation of action. However, they destroy or at least disrupt action when pursued at all costs. I've known and studied a variety of goal-

> oriented methodologies over the years. Even now I collect "goals" (a catchy label for ideas that pop into my head that I think are pretty good), piling them into an insurmountable heap representing "success." Therein lies the fable Satan wants me to believe: scaling the mountain of tasks is a worthwhile and beneficial endeavor. Frankly, when I fall into this trap, I experience persistent aggravation (because I'm not attaining my goals) and guilt (because I must not be the focused achiever I think I should be).
>
> This area of goal-setting and goal-pursuit is more difficult for me than any other, since it is the easiest trap for me to fall into and the hardest domain for me to successfully alter. My twofold answer to this dilemma is a careful scrutiny of how I spend my time, coupled with an assessment of my communication with God. God cannot honor what he does not ordain. What a tough lesson for a Powerful Choleric to learn! When he does ordain an idea, a task, a project, or a ministry though, watch out! Not only will he honor it, he will bless it. And, he will bless those working in it and those served by it!

Bev also found it important to have her goals meshed together with God's. She said,

> I try to have a prayer time in the morning, but I also awake with goals and plans for the day. If I have a goal to accomplish something, and he brings a special miracle to make it happen, or adds special richness to what he and I are doing together, it is a close time.

This illustration is so true of the goal-oriented Powerful Choleric. So much of his personality is wrapped up in what he "does or accomplishes." Bev went on to say,

> I've found that I do better with some organization. Since I have a good number of people I try to pray for each day, I did

> my list on the computer in larger print and put it on my bedroom wall opposite my head so I can read it from there. I find myself waking up praying, and I pray throughout the day. I think it is rather goal-oriented (that natural Powerful Choleric bent), but I try to make it God's goal that he is working out through me, and not mine that I'm asking the Lord to bless.

Bev has touched on one of the key areas of struggle for the Powerful Choleric in his search for spirituality: making sure his goals are from God and not simply goals he is asking God to bless.

Mae shared the following story that illustrates how she learned about goals the hard way:

> I gave my life to Christ because I had nowhere else to turn. I lay in my hospital bed awaiting the doctor's verdict, and my prayer was for God to do what was best for my children and me. He knew my children were most important to me. The doctor's verdict was positive. I gratefully and sincerely thanked God and set out to achieve what I thought was the purpose of my life. I was to see to it that my children were successful, according to my standards. My acknowledgment of God's role in the scenario was that I was not the decision-maker of whether I would live or die.
>
> My quest for the success of my children was an all-consuming goal. I made sure they were exposed to every available opportunity I could afford or beg. It was go, go, all the time. New challenges to brave and new horizons to explore. My Powerful Choleric daughter was eager to go along with it all and thrived. However, my Peaceful Phlegmatic son drove me to suicidal exasperation. He seemed determined to stand in my way and in the way of my goal. More than once I visited the psychologist's couch in frustration at the lack of control I had over this child. Much to my horror, his resistance was in the primary area of the quest for success. SCHOOL! This child was capable of grasping most any subject with little or no effort, was the most affable of

> his siblings, and the most tolerant in the household. He seemed oblivious to my bribes, rewards, threats, anger, or punishment. Nothing I could do made any lasting change in his grade point average.
>
> The psychologist and I were at wit's end. High school graduation was in jeopardy. As with my life, only as a last resort did I openly allow God to intercede and take complete control. God took care of graduation—and the maturity of my Peaceful Phlegmatic son into manhood. He is now one of the most tender, adoring fathers I have observed. He is a joy and God's gift to me. He is respected and loved by his siblings and co-workers. He is a supporter, a person who builds others up. And he loves the Lord. These are the things I believe to be important to God. My joy is in knowing that my son is under God's control, not mine. I am happy to say that by letting go of my goals and allowing God to take control, my son is also a success in the business world. I consistently remind myself of Mark 6:4–6. "Jesus said to them, 'Only in his hometown, among his relatives and in his own house is a prophet without honor.' He could not do any miracles there, except lay his hands on a few sick people and heal them. And he was amazed at their lack of faith." God dwells in me and I must give him control. Imagine that! God took control of my goal. Or was it his goal all along?

Evelyn Davison had a similar experience with her goals in life. She said,

> Through the years, the Lord has taught me some valuable lessons. One of those I learned from Henry Blackaby: "Be careful about the goals you set, they may get in the way of what the Lord wants you to do."
>
> When I committed my life to Jesus Christ as a teenager, I set a goal to have a perfect husband, perfect kids, and be a person that people could look at and see how great Jesus Christ is. After much adversity and pruning, I came to a better understanding of

who I was and who he is. I set more realistic goals. I had lived by the goal: work hard; work harder—then I set a new goal: serve hard; serve greater. I spent a lot of years believing that my family and others were dependent on me for their spiritual growth. I made myself their "Jr. Holy Spirit." Through much struggle and strain, the Lord taught me through his Word that I was not responsible for results, only for my example. That changed my life, and I changed my goal. I have it carved in wood over my desk and prayer bench. It is: He + me = we! While that is poor grammar, it is great theology. Most of us Powerful Cholerics think the world would not run without our pushing, shoving, stretching, and straining. God is sovereign and has a plan for each life. His plan for my life is different than that of my husband. Van is also a powerful personality, but he long ago recognized that God had gifted me in some specific areas where he is not gifted. Daily he prays, "Lord, help me be prosperous so that I can support all of Evelyn's ministries." So what we have learned after forty-seven years of marriage, is: He + me = we. That means we cannot do anything of value without each other and the power of the most powerful personality, the Holy Spirit. So our days begin with the prayer: "Lord Jesus, thank you for this day. Just as you give it to us, we give it back to you. You plan our day. We ask that you give us vision and vitality to live it the way you would live it." The powerful personality is a true gift to those Christians who are fearless, faithful, and fruitful for the kingdom—those who truly understand that his power is greater, and all the service and work must be done for his honor and glory—and no one else's.

We hope that as a Powerful Choleric, you can learn from those who have shared their stories here. Learn that while goals are a natural and important part of the Powerful Choleric's personality, it is important that our goals be God-inspired and not our own plans for our life.

Ida Rose says,

> I tend to be very goal-driven, but my goals have not necessarily been God-inspired. I've had goals such as finishing my master's degree and then my doctorate, but up until the last two years my spiritual goals have been either nonexistent or law-driven (i.e., pray an hour every morning). Now I find myself having goals like being focused on the Holy Spirit's leading when my four-year-old son is in the midst of his nightly suppertime temper tantrum. My primary goal in life right now is to know God. I still have other goals—like placing ten articles for publication this year—but I am not nearly as driven by them and they are subject to the greater goal of knowing Jesus and obeying him.

Those are some goals that all of us as Powerful Cholerics can embrace! What are your spiritual goals?

Powerful Cholerics are comfortable working toward a goal. However, because of their impatience—wanting instant answers, they are tempted to toss aside any method that doesn't give them the quick response they are seeking. Janet Allen is a Powerful Choleric, as is her husband, Jack. They use goal-setting as they seek answers for their lives. She told us,

> Goals are essential to a Powerful Choleric. Even the most disorganized of us has mental to-do lists and is frustrated when no progress is made on them! As married Powerful Cholerics, my husband and I have detailed, written goals for our lives (in seven areas), and we periodically quiz each other as to how we are doing on them. We rewrite the goals annually. We believe that this helps us focus on the important things in our lives and moves us toward fulfilling our purpose in life.
>
> On a number of occasions, we have given God deadlines. When we are praying for God to answer a specific question in our lives (i.e., whether to change jobs, complete another advanced degree, or move to another place), we have been known to say, "God I need to hear or see visible evidence of your will by such and such a date." And we continue to pray for an answer

to our prayer. God has almost always answered very close to the date we set! But we have also learned that God has his own timetable. He will answer at the last minute to show he is in control!

The important issue is to stick with the process until you find a way that works for you. However, somewhere in your process, the inclusion of time reading God's Word is vital to spiritual growth.

Judy Hampton stated,

> When, out of wrong priorities, I do not "seek first the kingdom of God," I soon open myself to deception and operating in the flesh instead of "renewing my mind" daily in his Word. Because God desires that I be conformed to the image of his Son (Rom. 8:29), I believe I have a lot of dying to self to do. My relationship with the Lord is stronger each year as I grow and mature in his Word and become obedient to it through the power of the Holy Spirit. The direction of my relationship (going toward the goal) is what is important, not the speed. Having a regular time with him has to be more important than anything else. When I don't do this, I suffer the consequences. There is "peace that passes all understanding" knowing the Lord is in control of my life. He is molding me and making me into the image of his Son, and my daily walk is a privilege, because knowing him is a privilege. Seeking direction from his Word and prayer gives me the equipment and perspective to walk in a manner worthy of being called his child. I take great comfort in knowing that when I blow it, he is faithful to forgive.

## Practical Processes

As a Powerful Choleric, Betty is action-oriented and impatient. Just sitting down to read the Bible for a set length of time, because it's "the thing to do," leaves her frustrated and unfulfilled. Powerful Cholerics must find a way to spend time with God that "works"—a way that produces measurable results in their eyes. Betty's strong desire to have a close relationship with the Lord has helped her to be persistent until she has found various methods that work for her. We will look at some options of how Powerful Cholerics might structure their devotional and Bible study time.

Betty was raised in a Christian home and grew up with the knowledge and expectation that a "real Christian" spends daily time in Bible reading and prayer. She was active in Youth for Christ in her high school days and even tried carrying her Bible to school as a testimony. However, carrying it to school didn't have much impact on her actions. And though she tried, she never established a regular devotional time. It was always hit-or-miss. For her, the denominational devotional booklets seemed trite and boring. Yet deep within she had the desire to have the kind of relationship with God that she saw in some of the older women in her congregation. She observed that these women each seemed to have a very rich prayer life. This observance precipitated Betty's lifelong interest in prayer.

## Prayer

Prayer is something that interests Powerful Cholerics because it is action-oriented. It can be practiced anywhere, at any time. So Betty began to listen to others when they prayed. She read books on prayer. As she heard about various methods of prayer, she experimented with them. When her children were young, another young mother in Betty's church approached her and asked if she would join her as a personal prayer partner. The two of them simply agreed to meet together on a regular basis to pray. They prayed for themselves, their husbands, their families (nine girls, from six months to ten years), and whatever needs came up. This practice turned out to be the major method of spiritual growth in Betty's life. She has always had a personal prayer partner since that time thirty-three years ago.

A scheduled time of prayer—to talk about what is happening in their lives, the lives of their husbands, families, and friends—meets the Powerful Choleric's need for "doing something." If you are a Powerful Choleric, you may want to try to find a prayer partner as a part of your search for spirituality.

Powerful Cholerics feel frustration when they don't immediately see an answer or a way to fix a problem. Betty says, "Identifying, recognizing, and talking about various concerns or problems together with my prayer partner has opened my eyes to see things from a new perspective." This has given direction to Betty's prayer life. As a Powerful Choleric, she finds it troubling to keep asking God to "do this or that" or to keep coming to him with the same requests day after day. Praying about a problem and talking about it beforehand helps the Powerful Choleric to be more patient. This process also opens one up to new insights. Sometimes Betty finds that she has to radically adjust her attitudes, actions, or expectations. Many times it has been her prayer partner who sees things from a clearer perspective. For example, Jan can ask gentle questions that may point out an attitude problem in Betty. Speaking words out loud to someone else sometimes helps us hear what we are saying in a different way. Betty has found herself recognizing hidden motives, underlying bitterness or unforgiveness, even as she is praying about a specific problem.

A prayer partner relationship is one in which two people come together as equals. It is not a mentoring relationship. It is built upon mutual trust and respect. It is something that grows rather than something that simply happens. It takes time to build a relationship in which each trusts, loves, and accepts the other. There must be a desire to be honest, vulnerable, accepting, tolerant, and loving. There must also be a willingness to believe the best about the other, even when the one can't believe it about oneself. Since control is a central issue for the Powerful Choleric, this can be a major hurdle in such a relationship. The Powerful Choleric needs to be aware of her tendency to want to control the time, method, and outcome, not only in a partnership relationship but also in her own private prayer life.

Being aware of motives can be healing and helpful to spiritual growth in the Powerful Choleric. Fear of losing control or of being perceived as not being in control affect the Powerful Choleric's method of public prayer. They may be more concerned as to how they are heard or viewed by those listening than they are by the sincerity and depth of their prayer. The Pharisee in Luke 18:11 might have been a Powerful Choleric. He prayed to be heard and to impress those around him: "God, I thank you that I am not like other men—robbers, evildoers, adulterers—or even like this tax collector. I fast twice a week and give a tenth of all I get." Jesus spoke harshly against the man, saying, "Everyone who exalts himself will be humbled, and he who humbles himself will be exalted" (v. 14). Remember that public prayer should be no different in style than your private prayer.

Betty has found various methods of praying that have fit in with her no-nonsense type personality. One of these is the increase/decrease prayer. This is a prayer for guidance and direction.

Betty finds she is often faced with decisions like whether to accept a speaking engagement or accompany her husband on a business trip. When there is no clear direction, she goes to God in prayer: "Father, if I am to take this speaking opportunity, increase my desire to do so. If I am not to go, please decrease my desire."

In another instance, Betty wanted to ask one of her daughters to attend a retreat at which Betty was speaking, but she didn't want to put pressure on her daughter or make her feel obligated to go. So she prayed, "Lord, if I am supposed to ask her to attend, then keep the thought fresh on my mind. If not, then let it slip from my mind." Betty has prayed this prayer many times. It has helped her find direction in a concrete way, something that is important to Powerful Cholerics. One of her daughters prayed this way when she needed to decide whether to list her house with a Realtor or try to sell it herself.

As a Powerful Choleric, prayer was the first step for Betty in establishing a daily connection with God. It was something that demanded action, and as we have said before, Powerful Cholerics need to feel that they are *doing* something about a situation. When the

Choleric begins to see results from their prayers, they begin to relinquish their need for control to God. They begin to feel they are in partnership with God.

Debbie Galloway has her own unique way of connecting with God in prayer. She said that she pictures herself on a big speakerphone with Christ. That way, she is not limited to a handset and can talk with him as she goes about her work. A Powerful Choleric's prayer is practical. She expects God to answer prayer practically.

Debi Diemling shared how her first direct answer to prayer came when she was asked to move to Washington, D.C., when her boss was elected to Congress. She prayed for God's help in finding a place to live. She only had three days in which to make her decision. She says,

> Each day started out with specific prayer for certain things to happen so that I would know that this was God's idea. I found a place to live, but what really blessed me was God's sense of humor and attention to details. The building was a high-rise, and I felt I should take advantage of a higher floor to enjoy the view. However, all the units had parquet floors, and I wanted carpeting. When I asked about an available unit, the manager said, "We do have a unit on the top floor, but there is one problem. The owner has installed wall-to-wall carpet." I moved!

Like Debi, Janet Allen has found that her action-oriented approach to prayer has given her guidance and direction for her life. She says,

> Action is the ONLY way! I believe that God gives us choices, and that there may be one specific choice that would be best for me to make, but if I mistakenly take the wrong path, I believe God can still make good things happen in my life. In other words, I don't have to wait and wait on God to make SURE that I have God's direction exactly correct. I make a decision based upon prayer, asking spiritual advisers, and reading God's Word. Then I go ahead with what I gathered as my answer for direction. I

expect God to act positively on those decisions and to fill in the details, and he does. I believe God steers a moving boat easier than a dead-in-the-water one, so when I believe that God is not blessing a particular path I have chosen, I quickly change directions and see if he blesses the new path.

When my husband and I moved to a new city (so he could attend school), we moved based on the knowledge that God had called him to move forward in his education and that God would work out the details. We moved to this new city after closing down a successful family business, and we took with us an enormous amount of debt in various forms, mainly the ownership of four homes. I was to be the new income provider. I looked at the debt service, school costs, etc., and, after putting together a new budget, figured that I needed almost twice as much income as I had before! I proceeded to cold-call every name I was given, and, in a way that only God could have put together, ended up with the most demanding, mentally challenging, stress-producing job—that paid the bills! I thoroughly enjoyed that job and grew spiritually because of God's provision. I believe that if I had not acted in faith and moved toward finding a good job, I would not have had the joy of seeing God's awesome work.

Shannon related this story:

A few weeks ago I was struggling a lot with being short-tempered, snippy, and very irritable, judgmental, and intolerant. I realized that I had not had devotions for about a week or more. I sat down that day and prayed for forgiveness. I asked the Holy Spirit to soften my heart and place the fruit of the Spirit in my life. Prayer and a focus on him every morning has made such a difference in helping me be more patient and loving. My husband says there is a marked difference when I take time to ask God for his presence in my life.

## God's Guidance

Because the Powerful Choleric has a need to control his own destiny, it is often hard for him to give that control to God and to accept the fact that, for now, God is seen and heard in indirect ways. We want clear answers—now! We are told that we will hear him as we read his Word, as we listen for the still, small voice in quiet meditation, or as we come before him in prayer. But these veiled ways of hearing and seeing God may not always seem satisfactory to us. While that is a normal human reaction, we need to keep reminding ourselves that our walk is by faith.

Thomas declared that he would not believe in Jesus' resurrection unless he saw his scars. Jesus told him, "Blessed are those who have not seen and yet have believed" (John 20:29). Thomas was no doubt a skeptical Powerful Choleric. Yet the Lord met Thomas at his point of need and satisfied his skepticism. And Thomas, though skeptical, hadn't given up entirely. He was assembled with the other disciples, perhaps hoping that somehow there was truth to what they had reported.

Philosopher and theologian R. C. Sproul was asked, "What, in your opinion, is the greatest spiritual need in the world today?"

Dr. Sproul paused, then replied, "The greatest need in people's lives today is to discover the true identity of God." He pointed out that most nonreligious people do not really understand the God they are rejecting.

Someone then asked him a follow-up question: "What, in your opinion, is the greatest spiritual need in the lives of church people?"

Sproul shot back, "To discover the true identity of God. If believers really understood the character and the personality and the nature of God, it would revolutionize their lives."[3]

The Bible was written as a guidebook. It is full of illustrations that show that God does indeed guide his people. From the very beginning, we see God giving concrete instructions to his people. When

Adam sinned, God told him what he must do next. Noah was told exactly how to build the ark. Abraham was told to leave his country and go to a new one that God would show him. Isaac was guided to find a wife. Moses was led to go back and lead his people out of Egypt. Even the instructions in Numbers and Leviticus are strikingly detailed examples of God's guidance. God was saying, in effect, "If you get sick, this is what to do, and this is how to keep others from becoming infected. If you sin, this is what you do to receive forgiveness. This is the way you are to worship. This is what you are to eat, and this is what you are not to eat." Practical, daily guidance is found through the entire Bible. In the New Testament, Jesus went to God for guidance in choosing his disciples. The disciples were guided first to wait until they were empowered with the Holy Spirit, and then to the specific places each of them was sent. The book of Acts could properly be called "The Book of Guidance," as it tells the story of God's guidance in the beginning of this new movement.

Isaiah 58:11 says, "The Lord will guide you always." Betty realized as a very young girl her strong need to know where she was going and her equally strong desire to control her future. This often brought conflict internally with her desire to also be a "good Christian."

She tells this story: "As a teenager, active in my church and Youth for Christ, I wanted to be a witness to those around me. I thought the perfect platform would be if I were to be selected Rose Princess from my high school. This was something most young girls in Portland, Oregon, dreamed about as they were growing up."

In Sunday school many years before, Betty had chosen Proverbs 3:5–6 as her life verse: "Trust in the Lord with all your heart and lean not on your own understanding; in all your ways acknowledge him, and he will make your paths straight." This was a verse that reminded her again and again of her controlling, skeptical nature and the need for her to let go and trust God. It was a source of guidance.

However, at this point in life, Betty really didn't want guidance, she wanted to be Rose Princess: "I remember thinking that I was to trust God with all the big things in life: who I would marry, what career to pursue, etc., but God didn't want to be bothered with the daily things. They were my responsibility. In truth, I didn't want God interfering with my daily life." She remembers, "Mother told me that she and others were praying that God's will would be done in the princess selection. I really didn't want God's will; I wanted to be princess. Somehow, I think I knew right then that I really wanted to be the princess for my own selfish reasons, more than to be a witness for the Lord."

God gives us guidance in his Word, but we have to be looking for it and be willing to obey what he shows us we are to do. This is where the Powerful Choleric's need for control often makes it difficult to hear what God wants to say. We read his Word with our own preconceived notions of what we want it to say. When this happens, we need to reevaluate our own guidance system. Often these systems have been put in place because of the traumas we have previously faced. We put up barriers around our hearts to protect ourselves from pain. We may filter directions and decisions through the philosophies that we have adopted to cope with life. We look for solutions from our own common sense or worldly wisdom and then seek to find Scriptures that will support our position. God desires to be involved in our daily decisions. He wants to guide us, but we have to be willing to let go of our control and follow his direction. For the Powerful Choleric, this often means learning the hard way. It may mean being removed in some way from our position of confidence and strength in order to learn new things about ourselves and to more fully trust God.

This was the case with Joseph (Genesis 30–50). He is an example of a brash young man who was probably a Powerful Choleric. He held a favored place in his father's household and apparently was a young man who believed in God and in himself. Joseph had a dream that he interpreted to mean that someday all his family would bow down to him. God had a plan for Joseph's life, but maybe Joseph was a little premature in announcing that to his family. *The Life Application Bible*'s Personality Profile says of Joseph, "As a youngster, Joseph was overconfident. His natural self-assurance, increased by being Jacob's favorite son and by knowing of God's designs on his life, was unbearable to his ten older brothers, who eventually conspired against him."[4]

His brothers naturally resented his pronouncement and conspired to rid themselves of this self-confident, power-hungry nuisance of a brother. Joseph, meaning well, went out to "help" his brothers, bringing them food and water. (Powerful Cholerics like to "help" others because it makes them feel powerful.) The brothers saw a perfect opportunity, and sold Joseph into slavery in Egypt.

As God sometimes has to do with us, Joseph went from a position of power and control to being a prisoner and a slave, with no power or control. Joseph was faced with a choice. He could have become angry, bitter, and disillusioned and turned away from God, or he could choose to assess the situation and find ways to make it work to his advantage. Joseph chose to accept the position in which he was placed and make the best of it. Like the Powerful Choleric he was, he quickly rose to another position of power, this time in the household of the prime minister of Egypt. The Bible doesn't tell us, but perhaps, once again, Joseph forgot to depend on God and began to depend on his own gifts and strengths. Potiphar's wife, when scorned, quickly used her power to punish Joseph. Again, he suddenly found himself removed from his place of power and placed in prison unfairly. And again Joseph was faced with a choice. He could let anger and bitterness overwhelm him, or he could seek to make the best of his situation and trust God for the future. Thrown back into powerlessness, he began at the bottom again. Once more, his natural talents and abilities led him to a place of prominence in the hierarchy of the prison. And the story goes on. Joseph is promised release, and it doesn't come. But Joseph continues to trust in the Lord. Finally Joseph is brought before Pharaoh, interprets his dream, and is given the responsibility of preparing the land for the predicted famine. Again he rises to a position of power. Because of the lessons he has learned in his positions of powerlessness, Joseph now has a clearer picture of how God wants to use his leadership ability to accomplish God's purposes. Finally, when he is reunited with his brothers and has the ability to extract retribution for his unfair treatment, Joseph chooses to let go of his need for control. He now understands that God is in control and has been through his entire journey. "God has sent me here to keep you and your families alive, so that you will become a great nation. Yes, it was God who sent me here, not you!" (Gen. 45:7–8 TLB).

Joseph went through a series of unfair circumstances. The Scriptures imply that Joseph was a devoted follower of God, and we may be tempted to ask why God would allow such terrible things to happen to him. Perhaps Joseph, with a Powerful Choleric's ability to lead, occasionally got ahead of God. Or maybe he was so wrapped up in the good he was doing that he missed hearing God's "still, small voice" calling him to come aside and spend time with God. Instead, we see Joseph being set aside from the busyness of his life and put in a place where he is forced to seek God earnestly for direction. "What's next, Lord?" he may have asked. In the end, Joseph became a compassionate, caring Powerful Choleric, tempered by the Holy Spirit through the trials and tribulations of life. Upon coming to the end of relying on his own strengths and learning to fully trust in God, Joseph was again placed in positions of power, but by then he knew and understood that this was of God. Joseph was simply the instrument God used to accomplish his purposes at that time.

God's plan for us is that we will grow in our relationship to him, and as we do, we will grow in wisdom and understanding. We grow in wisdom as we read his Word, seeking his direction, not his stamp of approval on our plans. Having grown in wisdom, and accepting God's sovereignty, Janet Allen says,

> As a controlling Powerful Choleric, I struggle with ANYONE

> else, including God, who wants to suggest how I should live. I have, however, fully accepted God as sovereign and do recognize that he is truly in control of my life. Powerful Cholerics know that they can do more than most people and tend to plan big plans. It is hard for me to include God in my plans. Once in a while I will remember the *Experiencing God* theme that if I can do it on my own, then God doesn't have to be involved, so then my plans get EVEN BIGGER! I try to give God lots of room to work and end up wondering if my plans are totally ridiculous, knowing that they look totally ridiculous to most other people. I still expect God to fulfill my plan, though!

Yes, we Powerful Cholerics need to learn to set ourselves aside and listen for his voice, disciplining ourselves to wait upon him.

## Hearing God's Voice

How does one hear God's voice? What does it mean to give up control and listen for God's direction? Can this be accomplished in the midst of our twenty-first century lives? "We have become a people with an aversion to quiet and an uneasiness with being alone," states Jean Fleming in her book *Finding Focus in a Whirlwind World*.[5] Yet the Bible shows us that Jesus put a high priority on times of personal silence and solitude. Let's look at his example to see if it is important for us as well. In Mark 1:35 and Luke 4:42, we are told, "Very early in the morning, while it was still dark . . ." or "At daybreak Jesus went out to a solitary place . . . where he prayed." Let's look at this from a Powerful Choleric's point of view. Jesus had people clamoring all around him for his help. He was able to meet all their needs; it was within his power. If we were in his position, could we ever justify pulling away to be alone? Powerful Cholerics love to be needed and even more to be appreciated for what they can "do" for you. Meeting other's needs gives us a feeling of control and power—both feelings that are quite addictive to a Powerful Choleric.

Going out for a walk, which is what Betty did just before sitting down again to write, is one way she has found to clear her mind of the pressing projects surrounding her. By intentionally setting out without a Walkman strapped to her waist, Betty is learning to do what Theophan the Recluse calls "descend from the mind into the heart."

This "descending from the mind into the heart" is a way of prayer or being that is more than merely an intelligent exercise of our mind. Often we become stranded in fruitless and trivial inner debates with God when we base our communication on our intellect. On the other hand, if we involve only our heart, we might think that good feelings constitute guidance or communication from God. When we combine our hearts with our minds, we open our whole person in unity to the awesome and loving presence of God.

However, Betty has struggled through the years with the frustration of not being able to quiet her mind and focus on the presence of the Lord. Henri Nouwen's writings have been very helpful to her in understanding not only that this is a common frustration but that there are simple exercises to help one focus. He says,

> The prayer of the heart requires first of all that we make God our only thought. That means that we must dispel all distractions, concerns, worries, and preoccupations, and fill the mind with God alone. The Jesus prayer (Lord Jesus Christ, have mercy upon me) is meant to be a help to gently empty our minds from all that is not of God, and offer all the room to him and him alone. When we empty our mind of all thoughts and our heart from all experiences, we can prepare in the center of our innermost being the home for God, who wants to dwell in us. "The kingdom of God is within you" (Luke 17:21), Jesus said. Then we can say with Paul, "I live now not with my own life but with the life of Christ who lives in me" (Gal. 2:20).
>
> When God has become our shepherd, our refuge, our fortress, then we can reach out to him in the midst of a broken world and feel at home while still on the way. When God dwells in us,

we can enter into a wordless dialogue with him.[6]

Author and speaker Linda Shepherd said,

> I have learned to listen for God's voice. Not an easy thing for a chatty person like me. I started the process by taking walks and making myself still before the Lord. As I walked, I would ask the Lord, "Is there anything you want to say to me?" Soon I began to hear his voice. It was not hard to recognize, because he spoke with such gentleness and love. Generally he would tell me things like "I love you" or "You are my daughter." I have since learned to call on him more often, whether I am walking, driving, or doing my chores. I now ask specific questions. Usually he answers. When he doesn't, that can mean "Wait" or "That's not your concern at this time." I have also learned that it is OK to ask him to confirm that I am indeed hearing from him. Sometimes I make mistakes, and sometimes I doubt my own spiritual ears, but God is faithful, and I am learning that I can trust him and his voice in my life.

Since Powerful Cholerics tend to live very much in the present moment, it is sometimes hard for them to understand that God is looking at the bigger picture of their life. They tend to want immediate answers to today's pressing problems. They are unlikely to see how events in their past are impacting their future. The future is something "out there" that they will deal with when it arrives. God's patient process of "working all things together for our good" feels like he isn't hearing or understanding our need to know what's happening now and how that fits into "our good." This may lead them to taking the situation into their own hands, often running ahead of God and usually ending up in more trouble.

In this next section, you will see many action-oriented ways in which the Powerful Choleric can draw closer to God and learn to set aside the need for control as she hears his voice and direction for her life.

## Journalizing

Journalizing may be one helpful way for the Choleric to step back and reevaluate what is happening in the present. Sue Stitt says journalizing is something she does occasionally. "Often I know that something is going on inside of me that triggers pain, confusion, anger, or even joy in my life. But I can't seem to put my finger on it. Journalizing makes things become more clear."

Powerful Cholerics often have trouble being in touch with their feelings, since they are more likely to base their decisions on logical thinking. Like Sue, Betty will often turn to her journal when she is feeling like her life is in limbo. The times when her speaking schedule is not completely filled or there is no deadline or project that is presently occupying her full attention, Betty is tempted to manufacture something to fill the empty space. Becoming aware of this tendency has made Betty see her need of taking time to stop and listen for God's direction. Writing out her thoughts and frustrations is helping her become more aware of her compulsive need for "doing."

Donna Smirl says that although her journal entries are spasmodic, sometimes two or three weeks apart, "journalizing is most helpful in keeping in touch with oneself, one's desires, goals, directions, etc. But it's like anything else: unless you are committed to it, good intentions don't materialize and produce. One must make the time and do it. It's so easy to get our priorities mixed up and keep busy on things that really aren't so important."

Journalizing is simply writing out whatever thoughts or feelings you are experiencing at the moment. It may be done on your computer, typewriter, in a specially designed "blank book," spiral notebook, or whatever scraps of paper you might have convenient. Betty often finds little bits of her journalizing stuck in a book or Bible or mixed in with notes on talks that she is preparing. In gathering material for this book, she was startled to find many different pieces of journalizing in her files. While she has several designated journals around the house, none of them are complete, nor are the entries in chronological order. She grabs whatever is handy when the need or mood for writing strikes her and lets her thoughts flow. The important thing is that she has discovered that journalizing can be a very helpful way to discover what is going on internally, as well as new insights as to what God may be trying to teach her in that situation.

Journalizing may or may not be something that you choose to do regularly. However, if you have never tried it, or tried and given up because you did not find it helpful, productive, or it was too time-consuming, we encourage you to consider trying again, spasmodically, without tying yourself to a rigid schedule. Look at it as an adventure, being open to simply pour out immediate thoughts and feelings without worrying about spelling, punctuation, or how often you write. You may discover a new way to become more in tune with God as you become more in tune with yourself.

## Solitude

In the midst of his busyness, Jesus pulled away to find a moment of quiet. Jesus tells us that he did nothing in his own power—that in everything he only did what his Father directed him to do. How did he know what his Father was directing him to do? He knew because he took the time to get alone and to listen. He told us over and over that he only did what his Father instructed him to do.[7]

Jesus knew the importance of disciplining himself to be alone in order to communicate with his Father. Dallas Willard makes this point when he says, "We must reemphasize, the 'desert' or 'closet' is the primary place of strength for the beginner, as it was for Christ and for Paul. They show us by their example what we must do."[8]

MaryLee from Palm Desert admitted that she didn't regularly spend time alone with God. She stated, "Maybe keeping a regular schedule of time alone with God would remind me that God is a part of my life in the good times. Then I might arrive at a point where he no longer needs to hit me over the head to get my attention." She went on to say, "God has been with me through all the terrible years; I need to set aside time for him." The independent spirit of a Powerful Choleric often takes God for granted when things are going well. It is our need to produce results that keeps us so busy that we can't seem to quiet our minds to listen to God, even if we do try to program time to spend in silence and solitude.

Sometimes silence and solitude have been mistaken for simply being alone, and being alone is one of our greatest fears. So we keep up a constant flow of words; we turn on our radios or televisions, anything to fill the emptiness and the quiet. We try to drown out the din and confusion that shouts within us by masking it with external noise. We fear what we may discover if we find ourselves silent and alone.

Richard Foster says,

> But loneliness or clatter are not our only alternatives. We can cultivate an inner solitude and silence that sets us free from loneliness and fear. Loneliness is inner emptiness. Solitude is inner fulfillment. Solitude is more a state of mind and heart than it is a place. There is solitude of the heart that can be maintained at all times. It is quite possible to be a desert hermit and never experience solitude. But if we possess inward solitude, we don't fear being alone, for we know that we are not alone. Neither do we fear being with others, for they do not control us. In the midst of noise and confusion we are settled into a deep inner silence.[9]

This is an area that Betty has found increasingly important in her own spiritual path:

> In earlier years of seeking God, I kept myself surrounded with noise. Good noise: Christian music, tapes of speakers, Christian radio programs—always on, while I worked around the house or ran errands in the car. When faced with silence, I always found some way to fend it off. Now I long for silence and solitude. I find I need both time and space to ponder what God might be saying through his Word, the words of others, or the circumstances of

> my life. But this transition has not been easy. I have found it hard to shut out my thoughts, plans, or worries. I did what most Powerful Cholerics do when they decide they need to make some changes in their lives. I ran to the bookstore and bought books that would tell me how to accomplish this discipline. Same old Powerful Choleric determination: I will make this work! But it didn't! Mostly, I have found that I have to "escape" somewhere away from my home in order to quiet myself enough to finally be able to begin to hear God's voice. I am still working on "giving myself permission" to do nothing but sit and be silent at home. I still fight that need to produce something measurable every day. It's hard to measure what God does in the silence and solitude of our hearts. Especially when there are many times when it seems he does nothing. Yet I'm aware that there is a subtle difference in me when I allow myself to experience a time of "intentional nothingness." These times are molding and changing me, and I find myself yearning, in the midst of too-busy schedules, for that time of silence and solitude. My whole being cries out . . . in fact, I think I need that right now.

It is the tempering of the Holy Spirit that is perhaps most needed for the headstrong, workaholic Powerful Choleric personality. Prayer and solitude are ways of opening our lives to him. Reading is another.

Business executive Fred Smith recently stated in an article in LEADERSHIP magazine:

> I've stopped calling my spiritual reading time "a devotion," but rather "a feeding time," for it is when my soul gets fed. It took me many years to finally come to what I believe to be a healthy menu uniquely fitted to my needs.
>
> We can't all wear the same glasses, nor can we take the same medicine. Just so, we have different personality and character traits that need developing or dwarfing. That means we must find the spiritual feeding that is right for us.
>
> Currently I'm reading from seven or so different sources. To

me, it's like eating seven-grain bread. Each source is contributing something I need, either in prevention, maintenance, or development. This includes the Bible, various writings of the saints, and short sermons by great preachers of the past. I find I feed best on those things that have lasted and that have produced the people I admire most.[10]

## Devotional Books

It is that desire to see and measure progress that propels Powerful Cholerics to find some type of devotional book around which to design their quiet time. While Powerful Cholerics are organized in their own unique way, they don't like to be locked into anyone else's schedule. Therefore, they are likely to pick and choose from different methods to find some way that meets their particular needs. This will often vary from month to month or year to year.

Powerful Cholerics are likely to be motivated for self-improvement. Therefore, books that are practical and instructional appeal to them. Powerful Cholerics may desire a book that has more depth than the one a Popular Sanguine might choose, but they probably will not want one as detailed as the choice of their Perfect Melancholy friends. In reading through the many surveys we received, we noticed that certain books were regularly mentioned. For the Powerful Cholerics, most were short devotional types that contained clear concepts and instructions.

Norman Vincent Peale was an author often mentioned. Lora Cramer said,

His books have things to do at the end of each chapter, and they keep me busy. Before I started having morning devotions, people would STAY CLEAR of me for the first hour of the day. I tend to be overly blunt and caustic when not fully awake. Now people notice the difference, although they are still careful. I notice the difference, and I like it. Since I started spending more time with God, I see more and more blessings. My personality improves, and my faith strengthens.

Several people mentioned devotional books by Charles Stanley, which are practical and helpful to them. Betty enjoys using the *Moody Monthly Devotional*, and many others mentioned this also. She likes this because it follows a theme every month, often going through a book of the Bible. The thoughts always have a practical application, which is particularly appealing to the action-oriented Powerful Choleric.

This book is not designed to give you more detailed directions as to what you "should" do to have a meaningful relationship with the Lord. NO! The very reason for this book is to set you free to find some way, any way, that will bring you into daily communion with him. What we are giving here are suggestions and examples of what others have found that have opened up their hearts and lives toward a fresh, growing, regular connection with their Lord. Each of us is different, even if we have the same personality. We are at different places on our path of life. Books that were very helpful to someone ten years ago may not be meaningful at all at this stage of life. Don't feel discouraged if something someone suggested doesn't speak to you or work for you. We want to encourage you to take the time to find something that does speak to you.

## Bibles

While devotional books can be very helpful in focusing one's thoughts in a specific direction, it is important that we do not rely on them to the exclusion of the Bible. With the wealth of Bible translations and versions available today, there is at least one Bible translation and study or devotional version to fit each person's particular need.

Having been raised on the King James Bible and often finding it too wordy and confusing, Betty remembers the overwhelming joy she felt when she discovered *The Living Bible*. For the first time in her life,

Betty got excited about actually reading the Bible. Before she had done it mostly because she knew she "should." Back when it was first released in the 1960s, her mother-in-law gave her the very first issue of Paul's epistles, *Living Letters*. She still remembers the day in 1971 when she first purchased the entire *Living Bible*. Even now, holding that original in her hands, she finds notes and underlines throughout that trace the lessons she has learned through the years. While that version has been particularly helpful to Betty in personal devotions, she has found that for deeper study she often refers to other versions. We encourage you, the reader, to spend some time in your local bookstore looking through the many different offerings in the Bible section.

Many Powerful Cholerics find that the Bible software programs that are available today are also an excellent tool to assist them in their Bible study and reading. Most software programs feature many different versions, along with various study helps, such as commentaries, dictionaries, and maps. We like the *Bible Explorer*, as it offers a great variety of helps and is available in a very low-cost introductory version. If you are a Powerful Choleric and do not already have a Bible software program, you might want to check this out. Take time to study the various formats, then talk to other Powerful Cholerics to find what edition meets their needs.

You may have heard others say that they have read through the Bible many times. You may also have tried to do this—time and again—and given up when you reached Numbers or Leviticus. Perhaps the persistence of the Powerful Choleric has indeed gotten you through reading the entire Bible, but without much understanding, clarity, or personal results. Betty finally discovered the most helpful way for her was to use the *One Year Bible*. She liked the fact that she had it all laid out before her—what to read each day, an identifiable pattern: Old Testament, New Testament, Psalms, Proverbs—clarity, simplicity, and a measured goal. A reading a day meant completion by year's end.

As Christians, goals become a marker by which Powerful Cholerics can prove their faith. Our friend Donna Partow bought the Bible software we mentioned. She and her Powerful Choleric foster daughter, Nikki, discovered that it includes a Bible reading program that tracks what percentage of the Bible you have read. They have had great fun watching the percentage go up and are competing with each other. Their goals are helping them stick with the program.

Barbara Anson also has goals regarding her Bible reading program. She says,

> Goals are also a part of my life. Perhaps one of the best illustrations comes out of the year when, because of other studies, my husband and I quit reading the *One Year Bible* together. When my most time-consuming study ended in May, I not only started reading that particular Bible again by myself, I set up a schedule so I could also get in the missed months as quickly as possible. That was three years ago, and although we no longer read the *One Year Bible* together as a couple, I continue to read it each year. Given my personality type (about evenly split between Powerful Choleric and Perfect Melancholy), you will know that if I miss a day, I then read the missed day *and* the current day. If I know ahead that my schedule is going to interfere with the daily reading, I often read those days in advance.

## Choleric to Choleric

Life and action, practical and persistent, this is what life is about to the Choleric. Their leadership ability tells them instinctively what needs to be done, and how to do it. They are the "Martha" personality, driven by noble motives, always occupied in fruitful pursuits. With so much to be done, it is easy to ignore the cultivation of the inner life, to find excuses to neglect Bible reading and spending concentrated time in prayer.

O. Hallesby says the danger for Powerful Cholerics is becoming

> . . . spiritually dried up Christians who outdo themselves in Christian work because they are not still long enough to permit themselves to be imbued with "power from on high," but rely on their own intelligence and strength.
>
> Therefore, Powerful Cholerics must put those same strengths into disciplining themselves to make the time to stop, look, and listen for God's direction in their busy lives. Luckily, Powerful Cholerics are made of stern stuff, and can discipline themselves to do so once they are convinced of the difference it will make in their daily lives.[11]

The advice we received from the Powerful Cholerics we surveyed concerning how they would advise someone like themselves to start a devotional time was overwhelmingly "Just DO it!"

# The Perfect Melancholy

# 7

*Be perfect, therefore, as your heavenly Father is perfect.*
Matthew 5:48

"I get so upset with myself! I beat myself up for not being the perfect Christian . . . not doing it the right way. . . . But . . . what is the right way? Who besides God is perfect? Why can't I be creative in my time with him? I keep doing the same old thing, over and over." This was the statement of frustration that Georgia Shaffer made to us as we queried her about a Perfect Melancholy's relationship with God. It turned out to be almost a universal feeling among the Perfect Melancholies that we interviewed.

Christian speaker Pam Christian put her feelings into these words:

> I'll never forget the day the Lord showed me, through my own words, how my prayers were filled with faulty logic and

lacked faith. We had been unemployed for over two years. I was bowed down under the weight of our circumstances. Not wanting to further add to my husband's or my children's worries, I sought a place where I could be alone. I chose my shower, turning the water on full force so that my sobbing could not be heard. Feeling abandoned, I cried out to God in prayer: "Lord, Lord, your Word promises that you won't give us more than we can bear. But . . . I'm not as strong as you think."

Even as I spoke those words, I knew that my logic and my faith were faulty. God is God, and his promises are *promises*. He wouldn't allow me to be in these circumstances if he didn't think we could handle this together. As the realization that he knew what was going on washed over me, I said, "OK, God, I don't know why I bother arguing with you anyway—you are always right."

But I've never forgotten that day and the piercing moment of realization that God knew, and was with me. That realization kept me going through the next two years of financial insecurity, during which we lost everything except one car, our furniture, and our clothing. All the assets that we had built up so carefully were gone. He thought I could handle it with him, so we did. God is always right, and his ways are higher than my ways and his thoughts than my thoughts, even though I'm a deep-thinking Perfect Melancholy!

## Self-Examination or Focus and Frustration

Pam Christian says she is still learning that his thoughts are higher than our thoughts (Is. 55:9). We found her story to be typical of the many Perfect Melancholies we interviewed.

Perfect Melancholies have a very deep nature, and this plays an important part in their relationship with God. In reviewing the many surveys we received, we noticed the constant repetition of self-examination in the Perfect Melancholy's life. Georgia Shaffer said,

> If I could wish anything, it would be to be able to see things as God sees them. To be clear about his will. It is one thing to do his will, but sometimes when I have prayed and things don't turn out "perfect," then I doubt myself. Did I really get the Lord's direction? Did I fail to hear or listen at some point? Basically, it gets back to my desire to be "perfect" in my relationship. So I have to work on that expectation. I am working on allowing the Lord to teach and show me how to be a Christian his way—not by my striving and struggling.[1]

Over and over again, we heard comments such as Irene Carloni's: "My relationship with God is good . . . but it always could be better. I have a hunger and a thirst to seek more knowledge about my God. I have grown through the years, but still I am not satisfied."[2]

Barbara Anson feels that "my relationship with God is a work in progress because I'm continuing to grow in my faith and ability to be obedient to God. I'm finally learning how to focus on God, his character, attributes, and especially his sovereignty, instead of my situation."[3]

## Head or Heart?

Perfect Melancholies, in their desire to be perfect, often value knowledge over their feelings. We found that many seemed to dwell on what a long time it has taken them to move from a position of head knowledge to a heart relationship with the Lord. Pat Sikora said,

> After the brief honeymoon period, when I first became a Christian, at twenty-eight, everything went dry, and my relationship with him was very "heady." I learned a tremendous amount over the next twenty years. I have a great deal of Bible knowledge, but I've lacked the power, the joy, and the feeling. I know we aren't supposed to live for the feeling, but I'd look around, and see everyone else having these wonderful, intimate worship and prayer times, and I'd be standing there cold and

alone. I tried everything. Different churches, different Bible versions, different studies. Lots of serving, doing, discipleship. Everything! Nothing worked! I felt like a stepchild. I felt less-than, not good enough, invisible. It was awful! I always felt like a failure. Yet I kept on leading Bible studies, writing Bible studies, praying for others, always giving out, never receiving—even when ministry was there for me.

Pat went on to tell us that she now realizes that a great part of her struggle with God had to do with her own past and the struggle to trust and feel love from anyone. She also realized that moving from knowing intellectually all that God says to actually believing and trusting her life to him in all ways means stepping out in faith. This sometimes looks very scary to her.

## Great Expectations!

Pat was not the only one who voiced this struggle to move into feeling a loving relationship with God. Becky Gilkerson said,

> I had been a Christian for thirty years before I experienced God's grace in a real way and for the first time realized how undeserving of it I am. Living within, and understanding more about God's grace, has brought me into a closer, more intimate relationship with him. I needed to learn it wasn't about me but about him. The closer I get to my Savior, the more I realize how much more there is to be experienced within this relationship. I pray that I will continue to be joyously overwhelmed at God's grace for me, and that I will always strive for a more intimate and closer journey with him. I am closer to God now than I have ever been. God has shown me recently in some very real ways how much he loves me, and that he has very special plans for me.[4]

High personal expectations and standards often keep the Perfect Melancholy from experiencing the love and acceptance that God offers to her. Her strong need for personal perfection makes her highly self-critical as well as critical of others. This focus on where she is failing rather than on where she is succeeding brings feelings of frustration and failure, often causing discouragement and even depression.

Pam Christian explained her feelings so eloquently:

> Growing up, I often experienced hurt and disappointment when other people didn't live up to my expectations or ideals. I was a normal kid. I thought everyone was like me! I couldn't understand why others didn't see importance where I did, or urgency where I did, or the need for total accuracy or to be "proper." I was often called "too idealistic," "perfectionistic," and people treated me with contempt and resistance. This wounded me greatly and caused me to withdraw. But it didn't change how I saw things. In time and experience, my "ideals" became tempered with wisdom and knowledge and compassion—perhaps because of the hurt and frustration I so often experienced with others, but definitely because of Christ.

This tendency to be "too idealistic or perfectionistic" was clear in the story Marjorie Chandler shared with us from her own experience. Marjorie was scheduled to be the seminar speaker for a large gathering of singles. Awakening to find a foot of fresh snow on the ground, she was sure that everyone would plan to be inside taking in the scheduled seminars. Her particular subject, scheduled right before and after lunch, was to be held in the chapel, which seated 400. Imagine her great disappointment when only a handful of people turned out for the first seminar. At lunch, she discovered that people had chosen to play broom hockey on the ice rink rather than attend her seminar.

> Surely those who missed the opportunity in the morning would want to come in the afternoon, I thought. I scurried to rearrange the room, restacked the overhead sheets, lined up the

handouts, checked the heat, the lights, the microphone, and I prayed. Yes, I was all set to go.

Fifteen minutes passed, then thirty. Maybe they are lingering over lunch. I looked out the windows; no one in sight. I walked the aisles and prayed. Slowly, I began to gather up my materials, still hopeful. Ten minutes later, I pulled on my coat and boots, turned out the lights, and wondered how to understand why I had felt called to be in this place at this time.

These situations are a real test for a Perfect Melancholy. They may vacillate between anger and hurt when others don't appreciate the "seriousness" or "value" of what they have to offer. Marjorie struggled with those feelings that afternoon as she walked the snowy mountain trails and allowed God to use that "wasted" time to teach her that what God really wanted was her availability that weekend:

Walking alone, I often talk out loud, sometimes shout, shed a tear, plead, question, express my frustration, anger, and sorrow, and almost always return with new hope. I had prepared and planned for a one-hour seminar, but God just wanted me to be present and available to be used anytime, anyplace, during that weekend. As I continue to speak, I hope I remember the things I learned that snowy weekend in the mountains. I learned not to expect things to happen a certain way, to minister as circumstances allow, not as I would direct, and to enjoy each day as it comes. God has a purpose in all things.

Pam Christian agreed:

I have often been perplexed as to why others don't see the "seriousness" of their behaviors or statements. Perfect Melancholies may be called perfect, but it must be in terms of wanting things perfect. I realize now that I have naturally very high standards. However, I have also learned that God is as forgiving and compassionate of my mistakes as he wishes me to be of others.

> Instead of being a misfit and oversensitive, as I'd been made to feel for all my growing-up years, I can use my gifts in a positive way of influence and service.

Pam has found her joy in life through teaching God's Word.

Perfect Melancholies, with their desire to "be right," not only search out other's motivations but are consciously aware that they need to check out their own ulterior motives. "I try to do too much in my own strength when I don't need to. Knowing that my strength is zero, it's stupid to rely on myself over and above God," stated Jim. "I know that I am not realistic when I evaluate myself on my good intentions, when I can't even know my heart. I need to operate in reality/truth by actively examining my motives much more than I do (though I do so quite a bit, desiring to be as properly humble before God as possible)." The inner struggle going on in this man typifies the constant checking and rechecking that is so prevalent among Perfect Melancholies. This often leads to unnecessary fear.

## Faith or Fear

> My desire is to give my complete self to God continually, but sometimes I really don't know how to do that. I fear letting him down, as I know I must. I fear that I don't understand his will for me in the way that I want to. I fear I am not tuned in as much as I should be, but this is not because of my not putting in the time—perhaps it is that I am not putting in my whole heart!

These fears stretched into the future, also. Becky states further,

> I knew the areas of my life that I hadn't released to God, and I was afraid of what I'd have to give up if I spent a consistent amount of time with him. The closer I get to my Savior, the more I realize how much more there is to be experienced within this relationship. I pray that I will continue to be joyously overwhelmed at God's grace for me, that I will always strive for a

more intimate and closer journey with him. As I begin to spend intimate, consistent time with God, he begins to change me and cleanse me and I willingly submit areas to him. Not having to carry such heavy burdens myself is the joyous result of turning these fears over to God. It is never a case of what I have to give up, but rather what God allows me to give to him so he can carry it instead of me.

Perfect Melancholies desire to have that strong, faith-based relationship that the Scriptures teach, but their own critical thinking keeps them feeling like they never quite measure up.

## Ministry Measured by Success

Each Perfect Melancholy expressed the yearning within that kept them seeking and searching to experience God in new and deeper ways. Along with their high expectations of what their relationship with God should "feel" like were their equally high expectations of what they felt he required of them in terms of commitment. This appeared to be equally divided between the need for "more knowledge" and "more ministry." Often what they "did" seemed to falsely define the level of their personal relationship with God.

A man in ministry who preferred to remain anonymous told how his spiritual failure was a result of his ministry success:

My spiritual failures are in part due to worldly success. This may sound strange, but my spiritual failures are also the result of spiritual successes. I work in the broadcast industry. The Lord has opened many doors and blessed them with success. However, my "works" are no substitute for relationship. I sometimes walk through too many open doors. As a result, I'm out doing many "good" things, but it gets in the way of the time it takes to cultivate a relationship with Jesus. It's not his fault. I will, however, testify to his mercy. I love him deeply. The Scripture talks about

> people standing before him on that day and calling him Lord. They will make their case that they did wonderful things in his name. The Lord never refuted their case. However, he told this group of committed workers to get away from him because he never knew them. The issue, then, is not what I do, but why I do it. The cart can't be before the horse. We should work for him out of our relationship with him, and not because we're trying to earn his favor. Sometimes I try to earn his favor. I also enjoy working too much.

This self-analysis is both the strength and the weakness of the Perfect Melancholy.

The measure of a person's ministry is often judged by the success it achieves. It is easy to fall into the belief that if we are successful in what we "do," then we are successful in our personal relationship with the Lord. Author and minister Derek Prince was quoted by one respondent as saying, "The hardest test that I have had to face as a Christian is based on my own experience of fifty years in ministry. It may surprise you, but the hardest test we are likely to face, and the one we are least likely to pass, is success." Unfortunately, with success often comes pride.

Sally is a Perfect Melancholy who experienced this test. Her story tells it best. Sally, a popular author and Christian speaker, found herself becoming more and more in demand. Her books began to sell very well, and she was getting more invitations for speaking engagements than she could fill. She became so busy in "ministry" that she found it more and more difficult to set aside time for personal Bible reading and prayer. It was easy to rationalize that the study she put in for each engagement or the time she spent in writing the next book or article was "really a personal quiet time." But as her popularity grew, so did her sense of self-importance. So many people were coming to her, seeking answers to their problems. Others were praising her for the wisdom she imparted. Sally began to believe her own "press releases." She began to think that God had given her a special ability to see and understand people's problems and was sure that if they would follow her advice, their troubles would be over.

The problem was, Sally became angry if others didn't see things her way. Her previous "servant's heart" began to change into the heart of one who felt she had certain "rights" that set her apart and above others. Her attitudes became demanding. Her expectations for special treatment, concessions, and privileges began to come before her concern for ministering to others. She began to want to control or reorganize corporate ministries in which she was involved. She often turned on friends and leaders if they didn't agree with her viewpoints, undermining their authority with negative comments. Slowly she found herself becoming estranged from longtime friends and ministry partners. Her popularity began to wane, and book sales and speaking engagements dropped off.

At first, Sally blamed other leaders, sure that they were jealous of her success and were probably bad-mouthing her. Then she blamed audiences that "didn't want to be spiritually challenged." Finally, Sally fell into depression and began to blame God. Then she came to the point where she basically admitted, "I can't stand myself." But God, who is so wonderfully patient with us, kept tenderly calling her. In her despair, and with much more spare time, Sally returned to journalizing. As she began to pour out her anger, frustration, fears, and loneliness, she found herself rediscovering the relationship she had had with the Lord before her tremendous success in ministry. She recognized and confessed her self-righteous attitudes, asked God's forgiveness, and began to seek the forgiveness of those whom she had criticized and hurt. Sally and God are on much closer terms now, and once again, she is beginning to be used by God to minister to others. But she now knows the danger of success, and she makes sure that her schedule never gets too busy for her personal, private time with the Lord.

## Rigid or Righteous

Sally introduced herself at a recent gathering of Christian leaders as "a recovering Pharisee." Pharisees were the religious leaders in the New Testament who prided themselves on knowing and doing more than anyone else. While all Pharisees are not necessarily Perfect Melancholies, the Perfect Melancholy personality is one who struggles with the issues of pride of knowledge and accomplishments. Pharisees were also noted for their legalism. The apostle Paul stated of himself in Philippians 3:4–14 that he was a Pharisee, most highly educated, one who followed all the rules, with many experiences that validated his authority. However, he was also aware of the dangers of relying on his perfect rule-keeping and personal accomplishments. So he reminded his hearers that all of this meant nothing without the power and presence of Christ in his life.

Legalism is a trap that can easily ensnare the Perfect Melancholy. Their deep desire to be perfect sends them searching for the "right" methods to grow spiritually. This can lead to a rigidness that says to be spiritual one must follow a disciplined and set pattern daily. If they succeed in following this plan, they may feel proud and somewhat self-righteous. However, if they are having trouble following what they believe or what they've been told is the "right" way to seek spirituality, it can send them into depression, promote feelings of failure, and even make them give up trying.

Pam Christian has resolved her struggle with the "musts" and "shoulds" by realizing:

> I know if I were to say I *must* get up at six every morning to pray, I could do it, but it would soon become meaningless—not at all genuine. I have a desire to always be genuine. I'm not afraid I won't be, it's just that I've known so many people who aren't. I don't want to be like them. They say you "must" do this or that. It seems that they "think less of your sincere devotion" if you don't have a daily routine. Routine for discipline's sake seems to

nullify the sincerity of the act. I feel less connected to God if I try to follow such a rigid routine.

Again, you can see the constant struggle of the Perfect Melancholy between her judging and condemning others and her fear of not measuring up to her own standards. Pam wants her meeting with God to be fresh and meaningful, not simply a routine experience, but she is somewhat afraid that if she doesn't keep a regular routine, others (even God) might question her devotion.

Oswald Chambers notes the danger of the rigid routine of the Perfect Melancholy:

> Your god may be your little Christian habit—the habit of prayer at stated times or the habit of Bible reading. Watch how your Father will upset those times if you begin to worship your habit instead of what the habit symbolizes—I can't do that just now, I am praying; it is my hour with God. No, it is your hour with your habit. There is a quality that is lacking in you. Recognize the defect and then look for the opportunity of exercising yourself along the line of the quality to be added.[5]

While that has been Pam's experience, others have found that if they don't set a routine and follow it, the day can go by and they never meet with God. We encourage you to experiment, to try new times or ways to meet with God. You are unique and he will direct you to the "perfect" way for you.

More often than not, Perfect Melancholies are likely to blame themselves if their devotional life is not what they think it should be. Therefore, they will keep striving to find a "perfect" way to meet with God daily, as well as the "perfect" method for praying, reading the Bible, and of fulfilling all the expectations they assume God has for them. Because Perfect Melancholies love schedules and organization, they are both the authors and purchasers of most of the devotional books on the market. Their disciplined example of the "perfect devotional time" is held up for the rest of the personalities to follow. The only trouble is that most Perfect Melancholies already have very full schedules, and they find themselves also falling short of meeting the standards that they set for themselves. Perfect Melancholy: Please relax! God loves you, accepts you, and wants to set you free to love yourself, imperfections and all, and for you to love him in return.

## Meeting God

Let's look at some ways that other Perfect Melancholies have learned to set aside their previous struggles and meet God in fresh new ways. Some must begin with schedules. Mark Reed, writing for *Decision* magazine, talks about his experience:

> Sometimes I'm so busy telling God what I need that I forget to listen to him. With all that goes on around me, it takes a lot of effort and concentration to hear God's voice. I have discovered some principles that help me to stay tuned. My listening time is scheduled in concrete. Nothing interferes. During my morning prayer hour, I spend time focused on God's Word—reading, memorizing, meditating, and journalizing. I remind myself during that time that God is speaking to me through his Word. After I read Scripture, I clear extraneous thoughts from my head so that I can listen to him. Every week I try to schedule getaway times when I go to the beach or lock myself in my office and spend time on my knees seeking God's presence. I find that I need to schedule everything in my life if I am to live by my priorities.[6]

Marjorie Lee Chandler likes schedules, too, but finds that the amount of traveling she must do often upsets those schedules and frustrates her. She has devised her own liturgy to start each day:

> I begin each day by opening my arms and saying out loud:

"This is the day the Lord has made, I will rejoice and clean my house (or other specific tasks from my schedule), and be glad in it." I follow this by a simple dedication of my mind, eyes, ears, mouth, hands, body, and feet to walk in peace. This sets the "stage" for my role in God's production for that day.[7]

Becky Gilkerson, who likes schedules, has had to learn to come to the Lord in new ways. As a wife and mother of three, a leader in her church, director, writer, and producer of children's musicals, she has had to adjust her times of meeting with the Lord:

> The various ways I come to him are intimate, spontaneous, and never stale. The spontaneous aspect I have had to learn . . . but as I have been less regimented and ordered about my prayer time, I have been blessed. I try to set aside time daily. If my mornings do not afford me that opportunity to be alone with him, I will come to him in the evenings when the rest of the family is watching television.

While scheduling is a problem that all personalities face, the Perfect Melancholy is more likely to differentiate between reading the Bible for teaching purposes and for personal growth. John noted,

> There is a big difference between studying for sermons, radio productions, etc., and taking the Bible into my closet of prayer with no agenda. For example, if you were to ask me if I've been studying my Bible lately, I will always tell you yes. However, that's only half-true. I don't feel like I've studied when it's only for the public side of me. I feel I've really *studied* when no one knows. This is another area where I often fail.

Georgia Shaffer has her own routine that helps her fulfill her desire to "stay in his will." She prays with her teenage son each morning before he boards the school bus, then after her Scripture reading and prayer-journaling, she looks over a few notecards that she has prepared through the years. These are favorite thoughts that have ministered to her in the past such as: "Gracious Lord, I come needing your strength in the weak areas of my life. May my fragile spirit be made strong through your healing power. So shape me, surely, subtly, and sweetly in your Spirit through your grace, peace, and mercy."[8] Or another from Oswald Chambers: "My devotion is not to humanity, for that causes me to be defeated and brokenhearted, but to Jesus, whom I love. I am serving Jesus."[9] These positive thoughts keep her focused on her purpose. She says, "Due to my experience with cancer, the recurrence, and the bone marrow transplant, I learned the truth of Isaiah 40:6: 'All men are like grass, and all their glory is like the flowers of the field.' I truly try to live my life as Christ wants me to."

## Praise and Places

When asked what made them feel closest to God, we found that all four temperaments connected through nature in some way. The Perfect Melancholy was more often seeking a quiet place, away from things and people: "Beautiful, peaceful surroundings, especially outdoors, make me feel close to God, particularly when I take the time to slow down and see the beauty he has provided," said Barbara Anson.

"The scenario that brings me into His presence so quickly," writes Becky, "is the majestic beauty of his creation—the heavens, the sunlit clouds, the snow-covered mountain peaks, the colors of fall, the freshness of spring, and so much more. The touch of his hand is ever present . . . the same hand that not only created all of nature, but created me, and then endured the piercing of nails for me."

While many mentioned specific places in nature, most also focused on the part that praise played in their coming into his presence. Jo Franz said, "In the mountains or at the ocean, actually any place where I am in God's awesome creation, I am overwhelmed with his presence and attributes. I am brought most quickly into his presence when I praise him, focusing on him, not me."[10]

Praise was often experienced through music. Diana James shared, "Coming into God's presence happens most quickly for me through the door of music. I often start my own private prayer time by softly singing a song with words that invoke an expectant, prayerful attitude, such as 'Spirit of the Living God, Fall Afresh on Me.' "[11] Marianne Lambert agreed. "Music plays a big part in bringing me into God's presence. Some of the worship songs and many of the old hymns help me to focus on him and what he means to me as my heavenly Father brings me to a sense of awe that he could love me so."[12] Many used praise music as a bridge to move them from the hectic pace of the present moment into the centering of their thoughts on God. Being in tune with the music calmed spirits and brought focus on God rather than pressing personal needs.

## Record Keeping

Perfect Melancholies as a type may be more disciplined in journalizing than the other personalities, but, even so, there was a great variety of times and methods used. Pat Daily shared with us this story from her life:

> About ten years ago, my devotional life had become as dry as the sand that whirls across the desert at the whim of the wind. Everyone goes through dry periods, I told myself, but the drought did not end and only deepened. Where was the exciting communication with God that the Scriptures spoke about? I consumed every book and article on the subject that I could find, as well as trying various methods of study to try to regain the excitement and closeness that I had felt before. Finally, having exhausted all of my own methods, I asked God to show me what to do to get to know him better and to love him more.
>
> "Write down your prayers in the form of letters" was the answer that invaded my thoughts the next time I sat down to read and pray. Being a prolific letter writer, the idea immediately appealed to me. That morning, I set out on a journey with God that

> has never again led me back to that arid desert where my thoughts drifted off to what had to be accomplished that day. Nor did I experience the tiredness that caused me to nod off before I realized what was happening. No more did I lose interest, close my Bible, and go about my daily business, having had no meaningful contact with my heavenly Father, even though I had been a Christian for many years.[13]

Sometimes those letters are full of praise and thanksgiving when all seems to be going well in life. However, there are other times when our letters to God express deep pain and frustration, such as this one that another friend, who also writes letters to God, shared: "Dear God, Where are you? What is happening? Why??? Why, God, didn't they find the cancer sooner? How can this be happening to us . . . now? What does the future hold? What course of treatment should we choose? Will he live or die?" The letter goes on, pouring out anger, disappointment, discouragement, and fear. In good times and in bad, letter writing to God is one way to keep your communications with him fresh.

Author and speaker Becky Tirabassi has been a source of inspiration to thousands of women on the subject of prayer. Many respondents to our survey mentioned how hearing Becky speak had started them out on the discipline of writing out their prayers. This is slightly different than writing letters to God, as noted above, in that you are writing the words that you would be praying. Barbara Anson wrote, "Becky Tirabassi's practical approach through her *Prayer Partner* is a tool I have modified to fit me, which seems particularly effective and helps to keep me focused."

Becky Gilkerson said that the most important step she had taken in her prayer life was to write out her prayers. "I found that I could concentrate and so often work through my willfulness if I began to write my thoughts and feelings to God. There is a much greater release within me, and God shows me many things as I write. He often turns my heart completely around. I previously could keep tuned into God for maybe a ten-minute prayer. But once I began writing, I found it was not unusual to write for over an hour. After such a time with God, I am usually refreshed, rejuvenated, and much closer to him. This one concept that I learned from Becky Tirabassi nine years ago, more than anything else, has changed my life!"

For some, these written prayers evolve into journals. "My file drawer is full of my prayer journals to God, begun in 1978," said Jo Franz. "I share my innermost thoughts, hopes, dreams, hurts, anger, requests, and praise with my Lord. I heard about prayer notebook pages in seminary, and from there, my own evolved into journalizing right away. I love sharing my life with the Lord."

Diana James said that as a writer it is natural for her to express herself in writing. Though she doesn't write in her journal daily, she finds that it is helpful to keep her on track when her prayers have a tendency to drift off in the direction of her "to do" list.

While some people use their journal as a prayer notebook, and others use it as a recording of thoughts and feelings, many have related how helpful it has been to look back and see where God has brought them through the years. Katheryn Haddad related her experience with journalizing in five steps:

> I can look through my journal a year or two later to (a.) see what was so important for me to pray about and what became unimportant; (b.) see what prayers were answered so gradually that I might have missed them; (c.) see how I interpreted a Scripture during one time of my life, and how I may see something new or different at a different time; (d.) see the common thread that keeps popping up in my life; (e.) see in writing what I hide from myself. If I didn't have these journals, I would miss being aware of how God is working constantly in my life, even when I am unaware of it.[14]

For Linnea Seaman, her journal has been a place to write the questions she has of God. Then, as she discovers the answers, it has been the place to record those. It has assured her time and again that God does answer prayer. It has also been a helpful resource to show her how God has been leading her.

If you have never tried writing your prayers and find that you have trouble keeping focused during prayer time, you may want to experiment with this. Perhaps it isn't prayer that is difficult for you, but expressing your deep inner feelings is your greatest need. Journals can be a very safe way to pour out honestly all that is going on inside of you. So many have shared that as they begin to record their feelings and fears, God opens their eyes to see things in a way they hadn't thought of before.

We encourage you to give journalizing a try, whether it is on your computer, in a fancy "blank book," or simply a spiral notebook or steno pad. The important thing is to keep your journal in a safe place, away from prying eyes. Part of the value of journalizing is the understanding that what you are writing is strictly between you and the Lord. Remember, He knows all about you anyway, so why not pour out your feelings, and let him clarify them for you?

One suggestion we received came from a person who hated writing anything by hand, but whose personality was such that anything written on her computer was compulsively edited. Since she knew that real journalizing is simply pouring out one's thoughts and feelings without regard to spelling and punctuation, she decided to mute her computer screen and simply type away for thirty minutes. This has been surprisingly effective, and she has been surprised at what she has learned about herself as she goes back and reads what she has written. Perhaps this might work for you.

A pastor in a large Southern California church believes so strongly in the importance of journalizing that his first sermon of the New Year is always on this topic. The church purchases thousands of 6 × 9½" spiral notebooks, and pastes a simple instruction sheet inside the front cover. This lays out the suggested plan for journalizing. With the notebook opened flat, on the left-hand page it is suggested that you recall what you did yesterday: decisions, feelings, observations, etc. The secret is to just start writing and not to spend more than ten minutes doing this. The last five seconds, rate your day on a scale of 1–10 in these three areas: physical, emotional, and spiritual.

On the right-hand page, choose a portion of God's Word and read it for five minutes. Then write your observations, thoughts, and insights for five minutes. Next, spend ten minutes in prayer, confession, thanksgiving, and supplication (requests). You may write these prayers or make notes on them as you please. Close your time with listening to God by inviting him to speak to your heart. Ask yourself, What is God saying? What are the next steps for your character, family, ministry? Spend about three minutes at this.[15]

The above is given as a suggestion that may help you find new vitality in your spiritual life. As with all the suggestions in this book, we are only encouraging you to try new ways of connecting with God, and none are meant to be "shoulds."

## Prayer

Mary was a servant in a bishop's home. One day during a gathering of prominent theologians, the question was posed, "How does a person follow the command to 'pray without ceasing'?" After a lengthy discussion, one of the theologians was assigned the task of researching the subject and writing an essay to be read at the next meeting.

Mary, overhearing the conversation, couldn't keep quiet. "What! A whole month waiting to hear the meaning of this text? Why, it is one of the easiest and best in the Bible."

"Well, well," said the bishop, "why do you say that, Mary? How do you understand it? Can you pray all the time when you have so many things to do?"

"Yes, sir. When I open my eyes in the morning, I pray, 'Lord, open the eyes of my understanding'; when I have washed, I ask for the washing of regeneration; while I am dressing, I pray that I may be clothed with righteousness; when I begin to work, I pray that I may have strength equal to my day; when I light the fire, I pray that God's work may revive in my soul; as I begin to sweep out the house, I pray that my heart may be cleansed from all its impurities; when I am preparing and partaking of breakfast, I desire to be fed with the manna and the sincere milk of the Word; as I am busy with the children, I look to God as my Father and pray for the spirit of adoption, that I may be his child; and so on; all day, everything I do furnishes me with the thought of prayer."

"Enough," said the bishop. "These things are revealed to babes and often hid from the wise and prudent. Go on, Mary, pray without ceasing."

While Popular Sanguines speak about praying all the time, there is an intentionality in prayer that the simple servant Mary illustrates is helpful to keep our prayers focused on specific tasks in our lives. Sometimes memorized prayers help us find that focus.

Pam Christian wrote,

> Prayer in my life is very important. But I don't like how I was taught. I was first taught to memorize "The Lord's Prayer"—which I can recite while thinking of a bizillion other things. Then I was taught that prayer is "conversation with God," but I wasn't taught how to listen. Then I was taught that prayer had to include some specific elements to be "worthy" . . . then that it simply had to be from the heart. Then, it's best to pray Scripture back to God.

Prayer seems to be a confusing subject for many. Most of the respondents mentioned the fact that they prayed in many ways all through their days, but their prayers were mostly one-sided. They talked to God all day about their concerns but rarely stopped to listen for his answers.

Søren Kierkegaard observed: "A man prayed, and at first he

thought prayer was talking. But he became more and more quiet, until in the end he realized that prayer was listening."[16]

Joan Beach discovered this when she and her husband were earnestly seeking God's direction for where they were to serve after he graduated from seminary:

> We had narrowed it down to two churches but just couldn't make a decision. The two of us took a whole day at a retreat center to do nothing but pray and read the Bible, seeking God's will for our ministry and our family. We worked alone, meeting at lunchtime and then alone again in the afternoon. At the end of the day we both had come to the same conclusion. We had peace about where we would go. We went with a strong and deep conviction that God led us to this place. That has been crucial to us when things have been rough, discouraging, or frustrating. We hold on to God's promise from 1 Thessalonians 5:24: "The one who calls you is faithful and he will do it." This calling came into focus through prayer—listening, not just talking.[17]

Of course, praying, asking, and then listening also demand that we be willing to do what we hear him directing us to do. Ouida Shelton says, as she has discovered personally, we should be very careful what we ask for:

> I ask God to direct me to whomever I can be a blessing that day. Often, before bedtime, an unpleasant personality will cross my path or call on me to listen to her oft-repeated sob story. This person may want to meet with me for lunch the next day. I anguish through it and return home exhausted. I sometimes want to say, "But not this one, Lord." But I go, and do, because I remember I prayed it into being. Who am I to pick and choose when God puts a person before me for his/her benefit and not mine?

However, Kathy Collard Miller reminded us that as a Perfect Melancholy she has learned the need to discern between an opportunity that is placed in front of her and the overall best use of her time in the bigger picture of what God is calling her to do. This is where we need to go to God in prayer for direction in each situation. James 1:5 promises us that if we ask God for wisdom, he delights to give it to us.

Prayer is practical. LEADERSHIP magazine did an interview with Henri Nouwen and Richard Foster on "Hearing God's Voice." One of the questions asked was "What is prayer?"

*Henri Nouwen*: "Prayer is first of all listening to God. It's openness. God is always speaking; he's always doing something. Prayer is to enter into that activity. Prayer in its most basic sense is just entering into an attitude of saying, 'Lord, what are you saying to me?' "

*Richard Foster*: "The problem with describing prayer as speaking to God is that it implies we are still in control. But in listening, we let go. Real intercession is what comes out of listening."

*Henri Nouwen*: "Too many Christians think prayer means to have spiritual thoughts. That's not it. Prayer means to bring into the presence of God all that you are. You can say, 'God, I hate this guy, I can't stand him.' The prayer life of most people is too selective. They usually only present those things to God they want him to know or they think he can handle. But God can handle everything. Prayer is thinking in dialogue. It is a move from self-centered monologue to a conversation with God."[18]

Perfect Melancholies, particularly, try to give God a "good slant" on what they are trying to do. Steven Curtis Chapman, one of the most popular Christian music artists today, is no stranger to prayer:

> I knew I wanted to write a song about prayer because praying has been one of the more challenging areas of my life. I feel like I never do it right. [A typical Perfect Melancholy reaction.] I've read books, talked with my pastor, and read Scripture about prayer, but I still wrestle and struggle with it. That's why I

> wanted to write a song about the importance of praying without ceasing, of walking through the day and having prayer become as natural as breathing.[19]

His desire to "do it right" has led to Chapman's song being recorded and used as the theme song for the National Day of Prayer.

Yes, prayer is talking to God all day, and prayer is listening for his voice. Jack Deere said that there are three essential characteristics for hearing the voice of God. The first is availability to God. People who are available to God see him as owning their day. Second, God speaks to those who will be willing to do whatever he says. Spiritual discernment is based on a willingness to do God's will. Third, to hear from God, we must embrace humility, for God exalts the humble. The highest exaltation God can give us is intimacy and friendship with him. Time spent in prayer with God creates that intimacy and friendship.[20]

One help to focusing more on making prayer an act of listening as well as speaking is to have one special place that you set aside as your regular place of prayer. The important thing is that it is a place both your body and mind associate with prayer. By having a regular place, you are saying to yourself and to God, "When I come to this place, I am trying to pray. Even if my mind is distracted and my prayers feeble, by my very presence here, I am at prayer."

Betty's son-in-law Bill Gaultiere has found his place in his morning jog:

> The other day I was taking my morning jog around the lake, and I was transfixed by the glasslike surface of the lake as it reflected the green trees and sparkled with the morning sunlight—it was a picture of peace, a gift from God that bathed me in his beauty. The Lord spoke to me, "Be still, and know that I am God." Sometimes I feel buried in the stuff of my life, everything from ministry responsibilities and relationship commitments to paperwork and e-mail! It's all good stuff, but sometimes I just

make too much of it and forget to take a step back and focus on what's most important. On this particular morning I was able to rest in God's arms of love even as I was breathing heavy and listening to my feet pound the pavement, step after step. Actually, the rhythm of my breathing and stepping helps to still my soul, getting me in tune with God. Being close to God in this way floods my soul with God's love, joy, and peace and causes me to burst forth with thanksgiving and praise to God for the ways he's blessed me.

These stories are meant to encourage you to look for new ways to speak to the Lord and to listen to him—especially a place and a way that works for you individually.

## Solid Ground

While prayer is an integral part of any growing Christian's life, the bedrock of our faith comes from the Word of God, the Bible. A survey taken by the Barna Research Group among people who claimed to be "born-again Christians" discovered that 18 percent, less than two out of ten, read the Bible every day. Even worse, 28 percent, almost one in four professing Christians, say they *never* read the Bible.[21] Perfect Melancholies may be more disciplined in studying their Bibles than some of the other personalities. Yet many admitted that most of their reading time was in preparation for Bible study classes, which they often taught.

"There have been times in the past when a personal quiet time has been lost for a year or more and preparation for Bible studies of one sort or another have taken its place. What has helped me to grow spiritually is Bible Study Fellowship, with its applications (they tend to hold me accountable), and the *One Year Bible* for a consistent Scripture-reading program," said Barbara Anson.

Her comments were typical of many. However, there was also the admission that reading as an obligation for a particular study tended to focus more on the goal of getting the job done rather than integrating the day's reading with the routines of a given day. Barbara admitted, "I don't think I *have* to have a daily quiet time. It's not like I'll be zapped if I don't. It's just that personal experience has taught me that my days go better if I begin by fixing my focus on God's Word and aligning my thoughts with his. It's a goal I want to attain."

Marianne Lambert shared this story from her own personal experience with the importance of reading God's Word:

> Our daughter was just beginning college. For over seventeen years, since a toddler, she had been having seizures that could not be controlled completely. In desperation, because they seemed to be increasing, we were referred to a new doctor. Upon examination and testing, it was determined that she had a brain tumor. At first, because of the location and depth of the tumor, they were afraid it would not be possible to remove it. Upon further testing, it was decided to attempt the surgery. We were warned of severe aftereffects: loss of memory and some vision loss. That day I read Psalm 20, and the tremendous promises found there helped me through those next hard hours.
>
> On the way to the hospital, our daughter gave us a box of chocolates, telling us that she had picked out two of every flavor so that we could each have one. This seemed very important to her. Her first question to us after surgery was "Did you remember that I gave you each one of every flavor?" We knew right then that she had not only survived the surgery but that her memory and vision were also intact. God's promises to me that morning had indeed come true.
>
> It is now eleven years later! These verses that were so very special to me that morning are still precious to me. God completely healed Barb, and she and her hubby are on their way to the mission field. I always think what I would have missed if I had not had my time with the Lord that morning.

While reading God's Word daily may not always have the quick results as illustrated in Marianne's story, putting God's Word in our hearts regularly prepares us for whatever lies ahead.

Connie Witt finds very practical help for her work from reading the Bible. "I work daily with students at risk, and I find reading the Bible brings to me a calming, patient attitude, which is helpful in my relationship with these challenging students."[22]

During a particularly frightening time, Georgia Shaffer found comfort and direction in God's Word. Having survived breast cancer by having one of the first bone marrow transplants, Georgia felt called to share how Christ brought her through those dark days. This clearly seemed to be God's will and direction for her life. The invitations for speaking were rolling in when unexpectedly, during her routine physical, an ovarian tumor was discovered. Two days before surgery, while reading her *NIV Study Bible,* she came to Leviticus, chapter 9, where the subheading read: "The Priests Begin Their Ministry." Those words jumped out at her, and she felt the Lord speaking: "Focus on my will. Begin your ministry." It took an act of faith on Georgia's part to receive those words when her future seemed so unsure. However, the surgery was done and the tumor was contained, and Georgia is once again busy in ministry and obeying her Lord.

Part of the value in regularly reading the Word is that God can and will speak to us from any and all parts of it. Generally speaking, Leviticus is not one of the more inspiring books of the Bible. Yet Georgia, faithful to read with an open mind, found God speaking to her through a subheading. For Perfect Melancholies, who want to "be perfect," the source for directions that never fail is found in regularly reading the Bible.

## Methods

Perfect Melancholies seem to be more drawn to scheduled and regular reading plans than are the other personalities. Some of their methods might be helpful to those of you who are feeling frustrated in connecting with God through his Word. Becky Thompson has found that her Bible reading is not only beneficial, it is "essential. It is food, it is manna, it is the breath of life for spiritual growth. It's my appointment with the King, where I receive guidance for the day, comfort, mercy, forgiveness, encouragement, and healing." She has made a special corner in her sewing room with a small table for books. She puts "shooter's ears" (earplugs) in to block out any noise or distraction. Besides her Bible, she finds that adding a special study book, along with other daily guides, helps keep her focused.[23]

A unique way of reading the Bible was shared by Katheryn Haddad, who for the past two years has written eighty chapters on the life of Christ:

> Although I have been a Christian since 1952, I realized that I never really knew Jesus. Each day as I wrote about events in Jesus' life, I would see his power, wisdom, determination, and insight that he used at that time. As I wrote, I found myself praising and thanking him with an overflowing heart. I can return to those special moments, the serendipities, when the sparks flew between us, because I have recorded them.

Perhaps writing out the incidents of the lives of Bible personalities in your own words might be a way for you to reenergize your spiritual life.

Most of our Perfect Melancholy respondents seemed to prefer study Bibles with good reference material. While writing this book, Betty roomed with a Perfect Melancholy during a CLASS seminar. Her roommate expressed frustration that she didn't have her favorite study Bible with her to help explain the passage she was reading that morning.

Favorite devotionals of Melancholies included the writings of Oswald Chambers, Hannah Hurnard, A. W. Tozer, J. I. Packer, C. S. Lewis, Dietrich Bonhoeffer, Catherine Marshall, and other deep thinkers. Perfect Melancholies want their thinking challenged. Sometimes they think the harder it is to understand, the more spiritual it must be. They like to read and reread their favorite authors. Jeanne Larsen says that she always dates the books she reads so that she has a record of when in her life they influenced her. "Is that not melancholic, or what?" was her comment.[24]

LouElla Dryer likes a variety of books to use along with her Bible. She has found many of Cynthia Heald's books helpful, and has also enjoyed Warren Wiersbe's series of commentaries on the Bible. She reads them along with the Bible. Henrietta Mears's book *What the Bible Is All About* gave her new insight and an overview of the Old and New Testaments. During one of her reading times, she said,

> The light went on that I was after "peace"—the gift and not the Giver. That really hit me, and I knew it was right. Another time the Word revealed to me that I was afraid of everything. Afraid! Afraid! Afraid! That was right, too, so I agreed and turned it over to him, because I couldn't change it, and I am not so "Much-Afraid" anymore. Though it took time.[25]

## View of God

Many Perfect Melancholies shared that through the years they had viewed God as someone who expected perfection from them. Debbie Minor said in response to our question about her view of God,

> At first, I viewed God as more of a Being to be revered in a sort of fearful kind of way. I perceived that I had to watch my p's and q's. If I didn't, he'd be sure to get me on track. That scared me. Through the years, I've become more tuned in to his grace. Stuff happens to us because we live in an imperfect world, rather than that we're always making mistakes and he's always correcting us. I think this came about because of all the rotten experiences that have befallen me. Eventually you get to the place

> where you say, "Uh-oh, I'm in a pickle again! God, I need your help, and thank you for your grace!" He becomes your friend instead of a Big Powerful Being who controls every aspect of your life, and you are this helpless sad sack. "What a Friend We Have in Jesus" has taken on new meaning!

Shelly Albany's view of God is "that he is overwhelming, bigger and greater than I can imagine. When I was young, I always pictured God as big and dark and faceless. Now I know that he is loving, forgiving, and patient."[26]

"Big and strong, regal and stately, gentle and approachable, very much like Aslan in the CHRONICLES OF NARNIA," was the statement of Pam Christian. She went on to say, "My view of God has changed through the years as I have matured. There's a lot to be said for growing older. Our spirits, unlike our bodies, are less and less wrinkled, spotted, or blemished as we grow older in the faith!" We noticed that most Perfect Melancholies had moved from viewing God as "out to get them if they weren't perfect" to someone who loves them in spite of their imperfections, someone who walks with them to help them become all he has created them to be.

## Perfect Melancholy to Perfect Melancholy

Perfect Melancholies had lots of advice to give those who were searching for ways to make their time with God more meaningful. Sonia Bryan thought that getting plugged into a small group and becoming accountable was most important. Debbie Minor thought, "First set aside a regular time when you are alert and as free from interruptions as possible. Even when you don't feel like doing it, stick with it; the rewards are so rich." Pat Daily thinks that using a prayer journal along with reading the Word is the best way. She suggests reading a chapter at a time, asking God to speak, and then writing what you hear. She also suggested that the *Experiencing God Work-*

*book* is a good way to get started. Georgia Shaffer, who values organization, speaks like a true Perfect Melancholy when she says, "Use your organizational skills of planning and set aside a time that works for you. Decide in advance how you want to use that time, and then have the materials, Bible, journal, devotionals, books, etc., right there."

Barbara Anson practically advised,

> Start with a consistent short time (at least five minutes), and increase it as you can (up to a minimum of thirty minutes). Try several methods until you find the one that works for you, and then *do it*! Keep what you need together in the place that works best for you. Allow time, even if it is only thirty seconds, to listen to God. Make your quiet time a dialogue, not a monologue (this is still the hardest part for me).

Pam Christian gave our favorite answer. She said,

> Take all the how-to instructions you receive, label them, and put them on an imaginary shelf. Then go to God on your own in prayer and ask him to help you find your own personal, unique way of relating with God—after all, that's what it's about, and there is no one like anyone else. [Yea, Pam! That's the purpose of this book.] I'd review all I was taught, and prayerfully determine what/how to implement the good stuff, and then build from there.

Perfect Melancholies are people who are orderly, conscientious, disciplined, precise, thorough, and analytical. They're perfectionists, who sometimes get bogged down in the details. Perfect Melancholies have a great need to understand how to do something. They want all the facts but get great satisfaction in getting things right. They are people who also get discouraged when it appears that they are misunderstood or unappreciated. "Elijah was a man just like us. He prayed earnestly that it would not rain, and it did not rain. . . . Again he prayed, and the heavens gave rain" (James 5:17–18). We are tempted to think that the people in the Bible were superhuman, untouched by their circumstances. But Elijah's story as told in 1 Kings 17, 18, and 19 shows us a different picture.

Elijah had been center stage in a drama in which God sent fire from heaven in answer to Elijah's prayer. Heathen priests and their gods had been exposed as phonies. Elijah should have been full of praise and thanksgiving. He was not. The evil queen's death threats sent him running. Fear drained him physically and emotionally. He was depressed and discouraged. Elijah said to God, in effect, "I have had enough, Lord, take my life. . . . Then he lay down under the tree and fell asleep." Elijah was feeling sorry for himself. How did God treat him? God did not say, "Elijah, pull yourself together." He did not say, "Depression is a sin." Instead, God said, "Be still, and know me." Many melancholies struggle with feelings of being misunderstood, unappreciated, or undervalued. God will always help you when you are trapped by depression. When you are unable to do anything, watch quietly for God's hand to move on your behalf. God has some lessons that can only be learned in a dark place.

Elijah's marathon run lasted forty days and forty nights. He arrived at the mount of God drained dry. When he exhausted his own strength, God spoke to him. God did not condemn him, but gently whispered the question, "What are you doing here, Elijah?"

After Elijah poured out his complaints, God brought healing by revealing himself. There was a wind, an earthquake, and a fire. These did not reveal God to Elijah, but in the silence that followed, God's whisper was heard.

God still speaks, often in a whisper. We must be willing to listen. We avoid stillness; we are afraid of it. We are too busy running to settle down and prepare our hearts to listen. Yet it is in the quiet place that God meets us through his Word.

God had noted all of Elijah's depression and discouragement. Like a true Perfect Melancholy, when the chips were down, Elijah felt as if he alone was standing faithful to God. God reminded Elijah, almost as an afterthought, "By the way, Elijah, there were over 7,000 others who did not bow their knee to Baal."

Perfect Melancholies, you are not alone. There are many others out there—different personalities with different ways to relate to God, but faithful to him in their own way.

Elijah met with God. He was refreshed, restored, and healed. Then God gave him the command, "Go back." Nothing had changed. Elijah still had the fire-breathing queen to deal with. God's "Go back" was grace-filled. He was giving Elijah a second chance.

Our God is a God of second, third, and fourth chances and many more. Perhaps you have tried to meet with God, and your meeting has not met your expectations. God is aware of your situation. He is not disgusted with you for quitting. But he wants you to know that he is with you, and that he can make you strong. Go back. Try again. God wants to be with you more than he wants your service. God loves you for more than your perfect rule-keeping. Perfect Melancholies may "try too hard" in their search for spirituality, trying to do their devotional time "perfectly," but God is more interested in simply meeting with them, whether or not the time is "perfect." Accept God's unconditional acceptance of you. The promise in Hebrews 10:14 can set the Perfect Melancholy free from his striving for perfection in the flesh by assuring him, "For by that one offering, God made forever perfect, in the sight of God, all those who [Perfect Melancholies, and all the rest of us] He is making holy" (NLT). God knows that the Perfect Melancholy, when finally faced with the fact that God loves him unconditionally, will put his hand to the plow and never look back (Luke 9:62).

Perfect Melancholies, we also encourage you to "cut a little slack" toward the other personalities. For God's promise to all of us in Philippians 1:6 assures us that it is he who accomplishes his work within us: "And I am sure that God who began the good work within you will keep right on helping you grow in his grace until his task within you is finally finished on that day when Jesus Christ returns" (NLT).

# The Perfect Phlegmatic

# 8

*Peace I leave with you; my peace I give you.* John 14:27

Peaceful Phlegmatics are by nature laid-back. They have a calm, well-balanced personality. They are often known as the watchers in life. Therefore, they may be overlooked by the other more dominant personalities. However, it has been the gift of the Peaceful Phlegmatic through the ages to be able to see the big picture in the midst of troublesome situations. Abigail, the wife of Nabal, is such a person. Her story is told in 1 Samuel 25. David was running from his enemies and had gathered with his people in the wilderness of Paran. Here he had been protecting the flocks of a wealthy landowner in the area. "His name was Nabal and his wife, a beautiful and very intelligent woman, was named Abigail. But the man, who was a descendant of Caleb, was uncouth, churlish, stubborn, and ill-mannered" (1 Sam. 25:3 TLB).

David had asked Nabal for food for his men, and Nabal had arrogantly refused. This caused David to react in anger, arm his men, and set off to wipe out Nabal and his family. We pick up the story in 1 Samuel 25:14–17:

> Meanwhile, one of Nabal's men went and told Abigail, "David sent men from the wilderness to talk to our master, but he insulted them and railed at them. But David's men were very good to us and we never suffered any harm from them; in fact, day and night they were like a wall of protection to us and the sheep, and nothing was stolen from us the whole time they were with us. You'd better think fast, for there is going to be trouble for our master and his whole family—he's such a stubborn lout that no one can even talk to him!" (TLB).

Abigail quickly sized up the situation and took command. She prepared a large feast and sent it out to David's men, meeting them on their way to take vengeance on Nabal. But Abigail did not tell Nabal what she was doing. (Peaceful Phlegmatics, who want to avoid confrontation, often act without telling others their plans.)

> As she was riding down the trail on her donkey, she met David coming towards her. David had been saying to himself, "A lot of good it did us to help this fellow. We protected his flocks in the wilderness so that not one thing was lost or stolen, but he has repaid me bad for good. All that I get for my trouble is insults. May God curse me if even one of his men remains alive by tomorrow morning!"
>
> When Abigail saw David, she quickly dismounted and bowed low before him. "I accept all blame in this matter, my lord," she said. "Please listen to what I want to say. Nabal is a bad-tempered boor, but please don't pay any attention to what he said. He is a fool—just like his name means. But I didn't see the messengers you sent. Sir, since the Lord has kept you from murdering and taking vengeance into your own hands, I pray by the life of God,

> and by your own life too, that all your enemies shall be as cursed as Nabal is. And now, here is a present I have brought to you and your young men. Forgive me for my boldness in coming out here" (vv. 20–28).

Abigail goes on to remind David that the Lord will surely reward him, for he is an innocent man, but if he murders Nabal and his family, it would be on his conscience. Abigail defuses a volatile situation with her calm, peaceful spirit and then asks David to remember her when he becomes king.

> David replied to Abigail, "Bless the Lord God of Israel who has sent you to meet me today! Thank God for your good sense! Bless you for keeping me from murdering the man and carrying out vengeance with my own hands. For I swear by the Lord, the God of Israel who has kept me from hurting you, that if you had not come out to meet me, not one of Nabal's men would be alive tomorrow morning" (vv. 32–34).

Abigail arrives home to discover her husband in the midst of a drunken brawl. Again, we see the patience of the Peaceful Phlegmatic. Abigail waits until morning to tell him what has happened. The Scripture puts it this way: "By that time he was sober, and when his wife told him what had happened, he had a stroke and lay paralyzed for about ten days, then died, for the Lord killed him" (vv. 37–38).

Here is an example of the wisdom and ability of the Peaceful Phlegmatic to see what needs to be done and to do it, without a lot of committee meetings or planning sessions.

While Peaceful Phlegmatics dislike direct confrontation, they will do what is necessary to keep the peace in the bigger picture. They are also peaceful and agreeable. Therefore, in relation to their search for spirituality, they are likely to agree with whatever is set as the standard of the group with which they are involved. While they do adjust to any setting, the Peaceful Phlegmatic has some experiences that are preferable to them. For example, the church or worship service is more important to the Peaceful Phlegmatic than it is to other personalities. Like being involved in a group study (which we will address shortly), the service provides structure and accountability.

The ideal service for the Peaceful Phlegmatic includes the quieter and more worshipful music. Linda Jewell told us that she "flinches" when her church starts the 8:00 A.M. service with a rambunctious song. She said, "I think of Proverbs 27:14: 'If a man loudly blesses his neighbor early in the morning, it will be taken as a curse.' "

They also like a service that includes time for contemplative prayer. Carol Johns, who is a combination Peaceful Phlegmatic and Popular Sanguine, told us about an experience she had in searching for a new church home. She said,

> I ended up at two churches simultaneously for about a year and a half. I didn't know my personality type at the time, but it explains what I was doing. For my personal, private, restorative times, I attended the Episcopal Church alone, at the early service, using the old version of the *Book of Common Prayer*. I felt very closely connected to the traditions of the church fathers. We entered the sanctuary silently, knelt beside the pew (you know that I just nodded), and prayed silently until the bells began to toll. This, and the weekly Eucharist at the altar railing served to me by Father Jerry, saying, "Carol, the blood of Jesus Christ poured out for you," was the doorway to worship every week. The regularity, the continuity, the personal relationship, and the peace drew me there.
>
> I left right after the service and headed directly to the Baptist church, where I was an encourager and honorary member of the worship team, Sunday school teacher, greeter, hugger, and assistant director to practically everything. There we sat around before the service leaning all over the pews, talking a mile-a-minute, hugging, laughing, and waving. There Communion was

monthly, with cups and bread in plates, passed around in the pews—more like a reverse offering than what I had experienced only an hour before. I referred to myself as an Episco-Baptist then, and I miss it, as I am greatly involved only at a Baptist church now. Oh, to find the balance in one place!

Like Carol, many Peaceful Phlegmatics mentioned that Communion was an important part of the worship service to them. Interestingly, in our surveys, the Peaceful Phlegmatics were the only personality type who even mentioned the importance of Communion. "Communion is a relational thing with me," said Evelyn. "I close my eyes and imagine that Christ is handing me the Bread and the Cup. I tell him why I feel unworthy to accept it, and he reminds me that he has dealt with all those things on the Cross. I come out of the time refreshed, renewed, and with a stronger sense of Jesus as not only my Savior but my friend." Linda Jewell agreed and emphasized that Christmas Eve and Good Friday Communions are her favorites.

Carol is single, so finding a church that meets her needs allows her to visit two churches, if that is what it takes. However, in keeping with the "easy to get along with" aspect of their personality, Peaceful Phlegmatics who are married usually settle for something that appeals to their more opinionated spouse. Speaking of her Peaceful Phlegmatic husband, Sharon Merritt said, "He is just now beginning to realize that people really do like to raise their hands and worship, and that it is okay." Since Peaceful Phlegmatics are universal responders, like the chameleon, the Peaceful Phlegmatic can be all things to all people. They adapt to whatever personality or church they happen to be in at the time.

However, if they have the opportunity to choose, most Peaceful Phlegmatics like a service that includes personal testimonies and some family time for greeting, hugging, and sharing news. This sharing of God's working in the lives of others was mentioned consistently throughout the surveys. Many spoke of how their lives were encouraged and challenged by what God was doing in the lives of others. Another mentioned services that included "contemplative" times or "prayer" times. Several mentioned that periods of silence during worship were very meaningful to them. The Peaceful Phlegmatic does not like services with hellfire-and-brimstone-style preaching, altar calls, or a rushed service. Many mentioned that it was helpful if the service included comfort and assurance. This "gentler" way of preaching, rather than the "guilt-producing" way, appealed across the board to the easygoing Peaceful Phlegmatic.

Evelyn commented, "I'm wondering if we Peaceful Phlegmatics tend to ignore or feel uncomfortable with the parts of Jesus that aren't our own personality (since he has all of them perfectly). We'd all like to think that Jesus is JUST LIKE US! That way we don't feel any need to expand and grow into being more like HIM!" True to their desire for avoiding confrontation was the comment: "No altar call—my most unfavorite thing about evangelical churches."

When thinking about the ideal church or worship service, a Peaceful Phlegmatic pastor's wife expressed the desire to see people being more concerned about what pleases God and what worship is to him, than about what pleases them. "I have seen too many arguments over the kind of music we sing and what color paint is on the walls!"

LouAnne explained her feelings this way:

> Sunday worship at church is unique because we worship individually with our Lord, and yet at the same time collectively. I love to worship my Lord with my husband on one side of me and my most intimate prayer partner on the other side. There is such power and unity as we worship, our lives so intertwined as we pray for our own souls and each other's. When we are individually being convicted the most, through God's spoken Word, those close to us usually know and are there with the touch of a hand or a hug during the message. My most ideal worship service is not only the individual parts that make up the service, but unit-

ing with close, intimate, Christ-centered brothers and sisters as we worship.

## Relaxed and at Rest

It was fascinating to see how many of the Peaceful Phlegmatic respondents spoke of seeing God as a place of rest or peace. True to their personalities, the Peaceful Phlegmatics seemed to not fear God, but rather look to him for comfort.

Sarah said,

> God presented himself to me as my loving Father some time in my first three years of life. My first memory is of crawling onto his lap each night to go to sleep. I have no recollection of anyone giving me that picture of God; perhaps they did. Crawling onto his lap to talk or to sleep, however, was the pattern of my childhood. I believed him to be my "real" father. God was always available for talk. I believed in and experienced his great goodness.

Anne Greer's experience with God is that while he is much bigger now in her perception than when she was a child, God is someone with whom "I feel very relaxed. Not casual, but at rest."[1]

The craving for peace comes through in Dr. Jerry Ozee's statement: "God wants us to have peace with all men, so God is peaceful."[2] Evelyn Sloat has found that as a pastor's wife she feels the demands expected of her have put her in a position of letting the situations of life take control of her: "God doesn't operate in that manner. He doesn't come and make demands that I spend time with him." This feeling of freedom in her relationship with God, though, has caused her times of meeting with him to be spasmodic. "Often more pressing things are always cropping up, and I'm always answering that call rather than his call to come and be restored. I always have good intentions. I'll go to bed at night and say, "Tomorrow I'll get up and spend time with God, first thing." I fight two battles with such a plan. I'm not good at keeping to schedules, and I rebel at the thought that my life will be dictated by sameness."

Relationships are very important to Evelyn, and she sees God in those relationships. "When we share our 'picture' of God with each other, we're expanding how all of us see God—who is infinitely more than any of us can realize."[3]

Others viewed God as being distant and impersonal. It was more of a boss/slave relationship, more religion than relationship. One pastor said,

> I did the things that needed to be done to at least stay on speaking terms with the Lord, but God was someone who was far-off, impersonal, and heavy-handed. One day I discovered that God really cared about me and wanted me to pray and study because he wanted a relationship with me. As my devotional life, especially prayer, increased, God became someone who was alive, though still not very personal or intimate. Then it became apparent that God wanted to be more than a friend. He wanted a relationship of intimacy with me. A place where we could walk and talk together, and where he would become relevant to every part of my life. This now makes me really enjoy being with him.

This discovery grew as this pastor moved from projecting the expectations he and others had of him onto God. He began to understand and accept that God had created him as a Peaceful Phlegmatic, not a Powerful Choleric, and that God loved him and wanted to use him in the realm of his natural gifts. Now he sees God as patiently working with him as a caring friend who gently chides and guides him day by day.[4]

Terri Geary had a similar experience in feeling that she had to be good enough for God:

> Many times I think I have to work at getting back in God's "good graces," or I have to prove to him that he is number one

in my life, even if I didn't have devotions that morning like that inner tape recorder tells me I am supposed to. I wanted to please God growing up, and I thought I was. Then my world turned upside down to the point that the real me started coming out. I began to realize that I had learned to pretend very well. The smile that was always there and the "cheerful" obedience to those over me were carefully placed in position by years of experience in pretending. When my husband became a quadriplegic in 1980, and I suddenly found myself with him and three preschoolers to take care of and raise, feelings I never knew existed began to come out, and they threatened the core of my relationship with God. Years of fearing God and pleasing him because I was supposed to weren't really enough to sustain me when it came to the nitty-gritty living of life after the 1980 accident.

But without boring you further, I would say that the many years that have followed became the basis for the beginnings of a transformation in my relationship with, and whole view of God and who he really wanted to be to me. He went from being not only the Sovereign God over me, controlling everything in the world around me, but my Refuge and my Comforter, who invited me to pour out my broken spirit to him. Generally speaking, I had not really experienced this side of him before.

Peaceful Phlegmatic Sue Roberts confessed,

For years my impression of God has been that he is a Perfect Melancholy/Powerful Choleric, and I needed to work very hard to meet his standard. In my present state, I am trying to create a new image of God—looking for a gentler God, who doesn't rate me on productivity but on relationships—which are easy for me because of my personality. My fears have always been that I wouldn't be good enough or disciplined enough to keep a relationship going. My Peaceful Phlegmatic side is not always very motivated. My relationship with God has a long way to go, but the good news is I am open to something new. I don't think that any relationship should be static—so it should grow closer or deteriorate. I want the growth.[5]

## Consistently Inconsistent

When we look at the personal prayer/study time of the Peaceful Phlegmatic, we found it to be consistently inconsistent. The "typical" (I say typical in quotes because our research has found that this style is far from the norm) thirty to sixty minutes of quiet time each morning was too big an effort and felt overwhelming. Sarah explained her experiences in these words:

> The early part of my adult life was ruled by "shoulds," being mainly motivated by what others would think of me. I was part of a women's Bible study group both in my church and a non-denominational small group. In both these settings, I received the message of God's expectation for my devotion. Besides corporate worship, tithing, and service, this devotion included a daily quiet time. (As a sidenote, the phrase "quiet time" is now unpleasant to me because of my association with this more legalistic period in my life. My time with God is frequently NOT quiet.)
>
> The model presented to me was of an early morning period of time—at least thirty minutes—in the same setting each morning. The time would consist of Bible reading, prayer, and listening. This was difficult for many reasons. I had small children with many early morning demands. I had trouble concentrating in the early morning, even apart from the demands of the children, and the whole set-up sounded confining to me. Guilt drove me to try to follow this model, but I failed more often than not. And it did not "feel" productive. I felt like a failure and somehow a fraud.

How many times have you sincerely wanted to have the meaningful "quiet time" about which you hear others speak? The longing to fit in, to be a part of the group, to meet with God regularly, to know his will for your life, lies deep within all of us. However, for the Peaceful Phlegmatic, the effort that seems to be necessary to expend in order to make this happen often feels overwhelming. One of the basic weaknesses of the Peaceful Phlegmatic is that it is "hard to get moving." Kathy Johnston honestly shared, "There have been times when I have run away from a devotional time from lack of ambition or the attitude that 'this doesn't work anyway.' But I always knew in my heart that wasn't true. Thank God, he always draws you back."[6]

Evelyn shared the same concerns:

> Many Peaceful Phlegmatics have "beaten themselves up" with guilt over the concept of NOT doing devotions in the conventional way, not being systematic and consistent in their time with God. (Albeit, they don't seem to feel guilty enough to actually make themselves develop this consistent time.) In my own life, I find that guilt is actually NOT a motivator, but a deterrent. "I'm not going to be able to keep to this time, so why bother trying?" And Peaceful Phlegmatics are so quiet and unmotivated, they are less likely to share that what is sold as the "norm" really doesn't work for them, never will, and that they've found another way! I'm not sure that their superior attitude isn't sometimes tempered with a feeling of inferiority because their way is usually sold as "sporadic" rather than inconsistent.

Popular Sanguine Vickey Banks told us that her Peaceful Phlegmatic husband . . .

> . . . is a man of uncompromising character and integrity. He is a deeply committed Christian and a highly respected leader. However, he has difficulty with such things as Bible reading plans and Scripture memory systems. As a matter of fact, he is now on the second year of a Read-the-Bible-in-a-Year plan! Brian feels it is important to stay consistently in the Word and therefore continually attempts to stay true to a system of Bible reading. He

says, "I've always wished it would get easier, but it never has."

Like Brian, Peaceful Phlegmatics can develop the discipline to stick with it, even if it never gets easy and even if it takes longer than it takes others.

Pastor Steve Hays told us,

> When it comes to my own personal study of the Scriptures, I do various things. I do not stick to one way or one specific time to study. Quite often I study a particular subject in-depth for a block of time, and then other times I study and pray here and there whenever I have the time. I am "consistently inconsistent." Being a minister, I do a lot of studying for the sermons I prepare each week, but I do not enjoy spending hours poring over books of Hebrew or Greek, coming up with my own conclusions. Instead, I will use commentaries written by specialists who have already done the research and come up with new ways to apply the truths and ideas of Scripture to our lives. I like to make the Scripture real and come alive for people.

While the Peaceful Phlegmatic does not usually follow the "typical" predetermined formula, many mentioned the idea of "soaking him in." This is often done through prayer and the reading of Scripture or Scripture songs and praise music. Chuck Alt loves the reassurance found in James 4:8: "Come near to God and he will come near to you." He finds that late in the evening, when everyone else is in bed, his time with God becomes a time of warmth, reassurance, and acceptance. As a Peaceful Phlegmatic pastor, that time with the Lord restores his confidence that no matter how hectic or frustrating his day has been, God is still there, loving and accepting him. It gives him the confidence to face tomorrow.

In fact, Scripture itself was mentioned more by Peaceful Phlegmatics than any other personality. Sarah confided,

> I found there were times I was drawn to Scripture, sometimes

for comfort, direction, reassurance, or just the need to sit beside God. There was no distinct pattern to these times. It would happen weekly but not daily—sometimes in the afternoon when the kids napped or sometimes late at night after everyone else had gone to bed. The times had no consistent length or content. There were times that were totally need-driven, during a crisis. I still do not have a daily time of Scripture reading. I memorized much Scripture as a child and continue to enjoy memorization. Scripture plays through my mind frequently during the day and when I awaken in the night. When I have a particularly worrisome matter, I like to type Scriptures related to the subject of the matter, print them out, and keep them with me to remind me of what God would say to me. In all these ways, Scripture ministers to me and draws me into God's presence. But none of these happen on a daily basis or in a prescribed manner. Rather, they flow naturally from the rhythm of my life and my great need for God.

Mary Seiber said, "I find that I want to spend more time than I have allotted to Scripture reading, once I get started. I just have so many things I want to do in the morning that I have trouble getting started."

Chuck Alt has found that his best study comes from selecting a passage of Scripture that speaks to the current concerns in his life. He will take a passage that has been helpful in the past, reread it, and then replay in his mind how he might respond differently in this situation. At the end of each week, he reviews the progress he has made, and sees what areas may need further study. He also enjoys using the *Thompson Chain Reference Bible* and follows the chain through a topic, summarizing the main point he has learned.

Scripture allows the Peaceful Phlegmatic to just "be" or to rest in his presence. Peaceful Phlegmatics like to ponder the Scripture, to meditate or contemplate—being devoted to a person, not a system or thing. Linda Jewell shared, "A friend gave me a prayer notebook, and

I've labeled one section 'Ponder Scripture.' I like to write out a verse or paragraph of Scripture and ask God all kinds of questions. I try to visualize myself in the setting, look up the meaning of words in *Strong's Concordance*, and try to see the nature of God and how to apply his Word."

In his book *Sacred Pathways*, Gary Thomas describes this person using Deuteronomy 33:12: "Let the beloved of the Lord rest secure in him, for he shields him all day long, and the one the Lord loves rests between his shoulders." Gary says, " 'Resting between God's shoulders' is the favorite pastime of the contemplative. He or she wants to enjoy God and learn to love him in even deeper ways. The role of the contemplative reminds us that God does not seek obedient, dispassionate servants, but rather a passionate love that is so strong it burns all other bonds."[7]

In their contemplation, Peaceful Phlegmatics tend not to look for new meanings or connecting texts but to quietly dwell in his presence. Dietrich Bonhoeffer said,

> The Word of Scripture should never stop sounding in your ears and working in you all day long, just like the words of someone you love. And just as you do not analyze the words of someone you love, but accept them as they are said to you, accept the Word of Scripture and ponder it in your heart as Mary did. That is all. That is meditation. Do not look for new thoughts and connections in the text, as you would if you were preaching. Ask, what does it say to me? Then ponder this Word long in your heart until it has gone right into you and taken possession of you.[8]

While it is easy for Peaceful Phlegmatics to "ponder the Word," Craig Brian Larson spoke of the difficulty of Peaceful Phlegmatics in moving beyond working in their heads to practical application in their lives and ministry:

> I do not like to organize and control things or people.

> Administration keeps me from what I love. I am an idea person, a word person, and a thinker more than a doer. I constantly analyze, question, read, explain, and try to understand. Thus I love to organize ideas, but not things—like money or files. Furthermore, I love to seek the Lord's face. I have to force myself to end my time of Bible reading and prayer. Gradually I have learned to administrate and organize out of necessity and a desire to be a faithful steward, but I usually do the bare minimum.[9]

An effective way of putting the Word into your heart and mind was shared by Mary Seiber. She learned this method from the Navigators. She suggested starting out by reading two to three Psalms a day over a period of two months, then using the CBA method of journalizing to put the Word deep into your life:

- C=Content. What does it say? Write down what you hear from what you have read.
- B=Best Verse. Write the best verse for you verbatim from the passage, citing chapter and verse.
- A=Application. Is there a command to obey, an attitude to adopt or consider, a sin to be avoided? What will I do regarding what I have read? Then write out a prayer committing to an action regarding what was read.

While most Peaceful Phlegmatics do not have a structured time of personal Bible reading or listening to God, they do seem to be more likely to quietly dwell in his presence throughout the chores of their day. Their relationship to God is often expressed as "spending a special time with a favorite friend. I look forward to being with him and love to prolong our time together."

Sue Roberts summed it up pretty well when she said,

> The most important thing to me personally in my daily relationship with God is just showing up and saying, "OK, God, I'm here and I know you are, too." I have tried to believe that he

is like a friend who doesn't care if I'm having a bad or a good day, but will just sit there and listen to whatever. [Don't ask a Powerful Choleric to do this; it drives them nuts.] Through the years I have seen that doing anything is better than doing nothing. So if my mind wanders a bit, it's OK with me—at least I showed up and said I wanted to do his will.

## Prayer

Prayer is given a primary place of priority in the life of the Peaceful Phlegmatic. "Prayer allows me to turn over to God what I am powerless to do," wrote Chuck. "It is good to know God loves me and will answer my prayer. I need to talk to God—no one else has to know what I say to him. That is good for me."[10]

Ceanne Richards says, "Prayer is my life's blood and gives back to me a tremendous peace in my heart and mind. I learned to pray by reading the Psalms and listening to others pray."[11]

Marilyn Heavilin, a Perfect Melancholy, told us about the attempts she and Glen, a Peaceful Phlegmatic, made to have devotions together in their early married years:

> Since I was trying very hard to be the submissive wife, I felt it was up to Glen to orchestrate this routine. It never worked. Glen wanted to put it off until evening, usually as we were going to bed, and I was always so tired that I fell asleep on many evenings during his prayer. I was more an onlooker than a participant. Several years ago at a couple's retreat, we shared our frustration with each other. Glen finally agreed that he would get up a little earlier in the morning, since I was already up, and we would have prayer together then. We take turns on the prayer part. We have discovered that we not only have been able to have time to pray about things that concern each other, but we have also discovered that this is a great time to just sit and talk about our individual day. We do not try to have actual devotions together. I usually have finished mine by the time Glen is dressed

and ready for our prayer time.

"I am still learning about prayer," said Barbara Amavisca. "I used to think that it didn't matter, since God knew what he was going to do anyway. But the years on the mission field have showed me that it is not about changing God's mind, but about changing me. When I pray and I see God at work, I am reminded again of his incredible love for me to allow me to participate in his work."[12]

Anne Greer sees prayer as an extension of relationship. It's how she learned to talk to God and to hear his voice. Suzzi Marquis said, "Prayer was always a part of my daily life. I awoke with prayer, went to sleep with prayer, and prayed throughout the day: in thanksgiving, intercession, and need. Prayer has continued to be like breathing: vital, continuous, natural, and spontaneous."[13]

Developing the habit of praying even in the midst of the most hectic times of life has paid off in solid dividends for Ceil Sharman:

> My adult sons and I sometimes pray on the phone, especially when they're stressed about something. It's an amazing way to keep in touch with our inner core and with God. This wonderful gift to me springs from their childhood, when even though I was often exhausted at the end of a long teaching/mothering/homemaking/wifely role, I'd read and pray with each of them nearly every night. What dividends God has shared from that time.[14]

Unique to the Peaceful Phlegmatic, formal or memorized prayers also provide a measure of comfort for many of our respondents. Earlier Carol John mentioned using the old version of the *Book of Common Prayer.* Many others alluded to the memorized prayers they learned as children: some as simple as "Now I lay me down to sleep" and others the specific prayers learned in Catholic schools. Sue Roberts was also raised Catholic, and said, "Written prayers were very important, but not necessarily meaningful. In my later years I have come to appreciate the value of both spontaneous and formal prayer."

Sheena Fleener told us about her Peaceful Phlegmatic husband, Pat's, prayers. She said, "He ALWAYS prays the same thing when we pray out loud together, especially when blessing our food. I thought it was laziness, but I guess he's comfortable with this prayer, and I'll get to hear it for the rest of my life. (Sure beats the alternative!)" Mary Seiber said she graduated from those memorized prayers to "learning to praise by singing and praying the words of the old hymns while taking walks in the fields behind my childhood home."

## Journalizing

It seemed that about half of our respondents admitted that journalizing was not something that they did. Even those who did were not regular with it. "I have started many journals, and I do write in them during stressful and confusing times," were the thoughts of Barbara Amavisca. "But for the most part, I don't do it daily. It takes up too much of my focus to get things down on paper, and then when I read it back, it sounds silly. But I have found it helpful when I am hurting."

Terri Geary uses her journal to capture thoughts and write out her prayers, but like her fellow Peaceful Phlegmatics, she doesn't do it on a consistent basis. She told us,

> I have tried to be formal in my journalizing, but have settled for getting rid of the guilt by writing when I have something I feel strongly about or that I don't want to forget. In other words, at this point I don't feel I HAVE to write every day, but rather when I feel inspired to hold on to something I have heard or want to think about later or use later. I have started taking my journal with me to church so I can capture what hits me and then have it right there where I can find it later. I have come to enjoy writing certain urgent-type prayers out so I can see how they are answered. I enjoy praising God in writing more than in just silent prayer.

Many Peaceful Phlegmatics who responded with comments like, "Yes, that's me," shared Terri's feelings. Evelyn Sloat remarked:

> Ironically, although I love to write, most of my journalizing is done via e-mail. When I learn something particularly special, I will pass it on to someone else. I will share concerns that I'm facing at the moment and discuss my struggles with staying a Christian when I'm surrounded by things that would pull me away (including a job that gets me too busy doing to be)! Once again, writing to someone else is much more entertaining and stimulating to me than simply writing it in a book that I may or may not read again. I also find that sharing the concerns and learning keeps me honest with myself and lets me get feedback on how I'm thinking.

Mary Seiber has another use for writing that is helpful for her:

> Sometimes writing letters to known people and never sending them is good. The process of writing becomes a prayer in which the situation at hand is presented to the Lord rather than to the person to whom the letter was originally addressed. Then it is dealt with in a far better way than burdening another with a problem that is best brought to the Chief Problem Bearer, our Lord Jesus Christ.

Suzzi Marquis doesn't quite call what she does journalizing, but has found that pouring out her thoughts on the computer in a mixture of talking with God, thinking through troublesome matters, complaining, and just getting thoughts out, has been very helpful in clarifying what is going on inside her head.

True to their laid-back lifestyle, most Peaceful Phlegmatics don't bother with taking the time or effort to either write their prayers or journalize on any kind of a regular schedule. So if this has been a source of guilt to you, we encourage you to let it go, knowing that

God, who created you, understands you and meets you where you are.

## A Sense of Accomplishment

We loved the comment in response to our question: "When you have a study time, what is it like? How frequent is it?" Evelyn's answer: "Step on my toes, why don't you! I still fight with guilt over the fact that I don't set apart a certain amount of time each day for such a thing. Study time is the more strenuous because it takes a concerted effort to stop what I'm doing and to spend time doing what I'm not!"

Most Peaceful Phlegmatics share Evelyn's struggle with guilt. As a result, like Diana James, many Peaceful Phlegmatics have found that participating in structured learning sessions, such as the Bethel Bible Study Course and Stephen's Ministry training classes, helps them keep disciplined in study. Sue Roberts agrees: "Structure is good for me, since it helps me not to have to make too many decisions. If I just do what the lesson plan says, I feel a sense of accomplishment."

Many Peaceful Phlegmatics found group study or prepared studies to be very helpful. The structure is good, as the decisions are already made, and doing the lesson plan provides a sense of accomplishment. Sheena Fleener, another Popular Sanguine/Powerful Choleric reporting for her Peaceful Phlegmatic husband, said, "Pat definitely likes structure in church and in a small home group. He always waits until the last minute (like outside the person's house in his car) to do his study. Without a small group, he really has a problem getting motivated to do any quiet time." Perhaps this stems from the Peaceful Phlegmatic's trait of staying uninvolved.

The Peaceful Phlegmatic particularly likes to see God at work in other's lives. Hearing the insights of others gives her new views of the Scriptures without needing to do a lot of personal study and research.

Others admitted that becoming involved in Bible Study programs, such as Precepts or Bible Study Fellowship, forced them to discipline themselves to read and study the Word. LouAnne found that her TLC group Bible study is a good way for her to really focus and study the Word. "I try to spend time each week on that particular passage of Scripture. I need to totally immerse myself in his Word in order to permeate my mind with praiseworthy thoughts and direct my actions. I have done the opposite and know full well the results." If you are not currently in a group study, we encourage you to get involved in one.

One of the methods that seems to appeal greatly to the Peaceful Phlegmatic is the practice of *Lectio Divina*. This is the ancient practice of Christian meditation or listening to God. The church has practiced this for centuries. Lectio Divina, or "holy reading," is a prayerful way of listening to Scripture with the express purpose of opening ourselves up to the transforming power of the living Word. It is a process of relinquishment and responsiveness to God's love.

"It's user-friendly, like rain falling on a dry and weary land. It deepens awareness of the Holy Spirit, is a calming influence, and unites Christians." This is the way Judy Nill described Lectio Divina in an article on it in *Presbyterians Today*:

> Although Lectio Divina isn't Bible study, it is a complement to it. When practiced in a group, Lectio is characterized by reading Scripture aloud, personally sharing the passages' effects on individuals' lives, meditative silence, and prayer for group members. Although individual Lectio is encouraged, group efforts result in close relationships with God and other members, and a deep appreciation and application of Scripture.[15]

There are four basic elements to this exercise. We share them with you as a suggestion that may be helpful in growing closer to the Lord:

- *Lectio*: Begin by taking time to become still before the Lord so that you are ready to give full attention to the living Word. Pray for the guidance of the Holy Spirit. Pick a short passage of Scripture. Listen to the passage as you read it aloud with an eager and longing heart, straining to hear the voice of God. Use all your senses as you hear the words on a literal level. Allow the text to come alive. Make no attempt to analyze, react, or draw conclusions; just gratefully receive each word.

- *Meditatio*: After a time of quiet, the focus shifts to active reflection. Read the passage again. Ponder what the Lord is saying to you. Is there a particular word or phrase that touches something deep within you? If so, stay with it. Let the Word engage your whole being. Interact with the Lord and allow the Word to touch your thoughts, hopes, memories, and brokenness. You may find it helpful to journal at this point. Allow the Word to address your deepest self.
- *Oratio*: The third step is response to God. Read the Scripture again, then move into a prayer of consecration. Offer to the Lord whatever within yourself you have felt him touch. You may be moved to praise or repentance, new commitment or deeper resolve. Consent to follow, and allow the Holy Spirit to transform your innermost being.
- *Contemplatio*: Read the Scripture a final time. Just BE. Simply rest in the presence of God. Remain wordless, still, and yielded, allowing the Holy Spirit to pray through you.

This may seem like a contrived practice the first few times you try it, but you will be surprised as you concentrate on only one passage of Scripture at a time, how many new things God can teach you.

Small groups, where there is a measure of accountability, are very helpful for the Peaceful Phlegmatic. As Barbara admitted, "I have learned a great deal from Precept studies, which have forced me to study harder and have challenged me. Right now I am in an accountability group, which has been good for the structure, the focus on right relationships, and for getting right with God. I also find that when I teach and disciple, it keeps me in line and on track as far as staying focused and being disciplined."

## Teaching

As Barbara mentioned, many other Peaceful Phlegmatics have found that teaching is an effective way for them to "stay focused and to be disciplined." Beverly Stone has found that taking responsibility for teaching parenting classes "keeps me on my toes and keeps me challenged to keep up my walk so I can be of help to the young parents we are working with."[16]

Evelyn has also found that she does better in being consistent with her study if she has a purpose. Therefore, she has taught *Experiencing God* and the Navigators series in a small group setting. "As part of my work, I write study questions for the International Bible Lessons, and I also teach a youth Sunday school class. Although I'm doing these things to share, I always study them as if God was speaking directly to me! Then what I learn, I feel I can pass on to others."

Vickey Banks told us,

> Brian and I co-teach a nearly/newlywed Sunday school class. One of the ways we have been able to do this together while remaining married ourselves has been to use someone else's material. Brian prefers this as opposed to creating lessons ourselves. Since Peaceful Phlegmatics tend to procrastinate, teaching together might prove too maddening for this Popular Sanguine wife if we hadn't found printed material we both love! This way, I can study whenever I need to and can fill in with all my colorful stories during the actual class time!

Group studies allow the Peaceful Phlegmatic to glean from the insights and views of others without having to do a lot of personal study and research. Hearing the teaching of noted experts on Christian radio, for example, is how most Peaceful Phlegmatics have learned doctrine. The issues are not of enough concern to them to spend hours researching. Much like the Peaceful Phlegmatic trait "I'd rather watch," many commented that listening to other people's stories or watching God work in others' lives was a source of instruction for them. The danger in this practice is that one can be easily led astray if one is not careful to check out how the teachings compare to the whole truth of the Scripture. So while we encourage growth through any means, we also warn each reader to look to the Bible as your main and final source of truth.

If, like many Peaceful Phlegmatics, you seem to have trouble establishing a daily devotional time, you can learn the truth of the Scripture the way Glen Heavilin does. He has found that listening to the Bible on tape while he is driving in the car has worked really well for him.

## Loving God by Helping Others

Evelyn asked,

> What makes me feel closest to God? Probably when I know he is using me to comfort or help someone else. Recently I went to visit an e-mail friend whom I had never met before. She told me, "I've been praying that God would send me a friend." I felt rather awestruck that God would choose to send me to her, but I felt confirmed that he gave me something that was especially put there for this relationship.

Diana James said, "I feel closest to God when I am deep in intercessory prayer. At such moments, my tears flow in an involuntary expression of my own heartfelt amen."

A creative phlegmatic says,

> My intercessory times consist of "reminders" I've placed around my house. A certain heart on the wall reminds me to pray

for a friend. I have Post-It notes around my computer so that I can remember the needs of my e-mail friends. Looking out the window reminds me to thank God for the blessings he has given to me. I try to stop and pray instantly when faced with a crisis, rather than wait until my set time and place.

This desire to help people comes from the fact that the Peaceful Phlegmatic has a great deal of compassion and concern.

## Que Sera, Sera

While the Powerful Choleric fights the idea of the sovereignty of God, the Peaceful Phlegmatic embraces it. The old Que sera, sera (Whatever will be, will be) approach to life aptly fits the Peaceful Phlegmatic, who is happy to go with the flow, assuming this is where God wants him. However, some Peaceful Phlegmatics can use this as an excuse for not taking responsibility for their own actions—or lack of them. The Peaceful Phlegmatic, by nature, avoids responsibility and stays uninvolved.

We want to challenge the Peaceful Phlegmatic not to use her belief in the sovereignty of God as an excuse for her own lack of responsibility. God has much more he wants to give and show her. In an article in *Decision* magazine, Elizabeth Carlson compared her spiritual walk to a walk she and her husband took recently in the English countryside: "At the bottom of the hill, our view was obstructed by cars and trailers and a crowded campground. The paradox of that huddle surrounded by a feast of beauty struck me as we walked up the side of the hill." She goes on to say that as they kept walking she began to tire and wanted to just sit down, enjoy the present beauty, and not try to make it to the top. Her husband reached for her hand after a brief rest and said, "Let's go a little farther." After a short climb, they reached the top of the bluff where the view was spectacular:

> I felt exhilarated at seeing the panorama that lay at our feet and at the large expanse of sky over our heads. I thought of the crowded campground. How often I live my spiritual life oblivious to the potential rewards of the heights above. I lounge in a convenient spot, content with the setting that I have created for myself, when there is much more waiting to be discovered.
>
> My world can be so hemmed in with clutter that I fail to see the spacious place that God has prepared for me. Then I need to go to his Word and ask him to open my eyes to the riches that he longs for me to enjoy. At times I have begun the ascent, but the effort of climbing has seemed too difficult, and my desire for comfort above all else results in an incomplete and disappointing perspective of God.
>
> How grateful I am that the Holy Spirit keeps saying to me, "Come up higher!" As I take his hand, he leads me upward, strengthens my stride, and "enables me to stand on the heights."[17]

God wants to move you higher and closer to himself. He is waiting for you, and the effort expended will be well rewarded.

The Peaceful Phlegmatic resigns himself quite easily to his fate. He is likely to adhere to whatever position requires the least exertion. If the Powerful Choleric, or the Perfect Melancholy, firmly insist that there is just one way to have a meaningful "quiet time," the Peaceful Phlegmatic will nod in agreement and go on doing it his own way. He won't take the time or energy to argue, nor does he get too caught up in self-condemnation.

The danger in this is that the Peaceful Phlegmatic is well protected from the accusations of his conscience. His calm, clear intellect helps him skillfully parry all strokes from the sword of truth, defending his own code of morality and godliness as the only one that makes sense. This lends itself to a tendency toward self-righteousness and a feeling of superiority. The ability of the Peaceful Phlegmatic to sit back and observe with detachment the conflicts and conversations of the other temperaments, without feeling any need to become involved, makes it easy for him to consider himself above average in morality. So while the Perfect Melancholy tends to spend lots of time in self-examination, the Peaceful Phlegmatic is content to live a rather "anonymous" Christian life.

According to O. Hallesby, in his book *Temperament and the Christian Faith*,

> The Peaceful Phlegmatic is easily tempted to become an "anonymous" Christian because he wants to create the least possible disturbance, and because he realizes that an open confession will cause inconvenience. He must first of all struggle against his indolence, for it is this weakness that tempts him to compromise with his ideals and feel satisfied with lowered standards. Therefore, the Christian life of a phlegmatic may look like a blameless, well-balanced life, which nevertheless conceals egotism and sins of omission, the really special sins of a Peaceful Phlegmatic.[18]

## Peaceful Phlegmatic to Peaceful Phlegmatic

Much of the advice Peaceful Phlegmatics offered to their brothers and sisters involved making a commitment of time. Anne Greer thinks it important "to be intentional, but not legalistic. Give him priority." For example, Anne doesn't allow herself to read magazines or the paper until she has read the Scriptures. She does the same with television. It is a discipline, but she reminds us not to feel down on ourselves when we fail, because we all will. Most important of all, she believes, is to meet with God out of love, not obligation.

Barbara agrees with Anne. "When we don't take that step and discipline ourselves to set apart time with God, it is hard for God to get our attention in these busy lives of ours. There are so many things that clamor for our attention. If there is not an intentional discipline,

I don't see any way that it can happen."

Ken Klassen stated it strongly: "If you don't MAKE TIME, you won't take time. Ask God to give you a heart that beats like his heart, and to give you a love for him—a heart to 'pant for him as a deer pants for the water.' " Encouragers that they are, the Peaceful Phlegmatics, even those who admitted struggling so much, said, "Keep trying; find a time that works best for your schedule. Morning is best, to get a good start on the day, but if another time works better, then take advantage of it." Diana James suggested, "Find a time that best suits your circumstances and your habits, when you can be alone in a quiet place. Commit even a few minutes each day to thinking about God, reading Scripture, and praying. Don't give up, even if it doesn't work out at first. Keep trying, and God will bless your efforts."

Pastor Chuck Alt reminds us to "not be in a hurry to cover a book of the Bible. Read until you find a nugget of gold that speaks to your heart. Meditate on it; receive its full meaning. Apply it to your past so you can use it in the future. Make sure you find a place where no one can disturb you."

"Set a time and place when you can have a few minutes alone with God. KEEP the appointment, as one with your very best friend, because it is such an appointment," said Mary Seiber. "Remember, your Friend wants to meet with you, too, and give him time to speak when you do meet. If you miss an appointment with your friend, you call her, right? So if you miss your quiet time, call on God during the day and promise to do better next time." Linda Jewell also encouraged her fellow Peaceful Phlegmatics to find a special place, a "sacred place" for your quiet time. She told us,

> Every morning I go to my office, open the drapes, light a candle, sing a song, sit in my little brown rocking chair, write out my prayers, and ponder the Scriptures. On cool mornings, I wrap up in a lap quilt from my older sister and a soft blanket from my mother. My view is of bookcases, a tall, brass candlestick from

my older sister, a needlework pillow that says "Sisters Are Friends Forever" from my younger sister. On top of the shorter bookcase, I have a small lamp with a handmade shade, a few precious-to-me books on letters, a framed Scripture: "Be still, and know that I am God" (Psalm 46:10). Through the window, I can see ivy on the wall, branches of a fig tree, and the night change to day with each sunrise.

Obviously, time is an element with which the Peaceful Phlegmatic struggles. Another issue that we saw time and time again dealt with the idea of accepting differences. Since our questions contained the words "meaningful, regular time with God," Suzzi Marquis advised, "Accept that 'meaningful' and 'regular' will have a different meaning in each season of life. Trust that in seeking God, he will be found. And seek him in the reality of who you are. Trust that God designed you uniquely, and in his vastness he has a great desire for diversity that includes each of us." Along the same lines, Terri Geary advised, "BE REAL. Ask God to help you stop any pretending you might have developed over the years and JUST BE REAL."

Sue Roberts gives a good reminder when she says, "I would advise anyone with my personality to remember not to compare herself with the Perfect Melancholy. I want to keep reminding myself that God made me laid-back and accepts me that way. I like to focus on the dependable part of my personality: Just show up."

Pastor Steve Hays says, "My best advice for Peaceful Phlegmatics is to vary your routine. Do not feel as though you are a failure because you do not have the same set time every day for study and prayer. We Peaceful Phlegmatics tend to enjoy the variety as long as we are consistently spending time with our Lord."

More advice related to dealing with other people: Ceanne Richards says, "Keep your eyes off of yourself. Work at what it is to walk in another's shoes. Be compassionate and loving; show honor and respect to all people."

O. Hallesby encourages the Peaceful Phlegmatic with these words:

> His love of peace and harmony makes him exceptionally good in dealing with many different kinds of people. His serenity and poise have a unifying and healing influence. The Christian phlegmatic is very valuable in the church. His Christian life will be characterized by clarity and calm. He truly possesses the "sound mind," which the apostle speaks of in 2 Timothy 1:7.
>
> If the phlegmatic will begin to practice some loving service in his everyday life, his heart will gradually open and he will become more and more aware of the needs and wants of others. He will then begin to experience a joy far surpassing the purely negative pleasure of living an indolent and undisturbed life. He will feel the pure joy and delight of making others happy. But it takes a hard struggle. He may suffer many defeats, for this easygoing nature is strong. He may never become very enterprising, but this does not mean he will not work. He is an excellent leader. No one has better administrative abilities than he.[19]

Because of the calm outlook of Peaceful Phlegmatics, they can see people and situations dispassionately. This gives them the ability to look at the big picture and see what really needs to be done. One of their strengths is the ability to pull together diverse groups of people and put their various talents to work where they are most needed—to mediate problems. Linda Jewell said, "God often has me in the role as a peacemaker—helping one warring faction see the other's viewpoint and finding common ground, to calm things down instead of stirring them up."

Once they make up their minds to take on a project, Peaceful Phlegmatics have the patience to see it through. They also possess toughness and perseverance that won't give up until the goal is reached.

Evelyn Sloat had a number of good suggestions. We present them to you exactly as she wrote them:

*First,* don't respond out of guilt. For years I tried to do devotions because I was supposed to, and I used guilt as the motivating factor. It didn't work and made me feel badly about God and about myself.

*Second,* realize that God loves you for who you are! He gave you this personality and he wants you to worship him through your personality. He has plans for you just the way you are!

*Third,* devote time to him BECAUSE you love him! Think of him as a friend, not a dictator or the Judge ready to squash you down. Allow your devotion to him to flow from you naturally. Don't be boxed into thinking there is only one way to be devoted to him. Keep trying different things. See what works and what doesn't. If you get bored, don't be afraid to change. Ask God to show you another way! Don't do it the same every day. Think of yourself as devoted to a Person, not a system or a thing. My friends expect the unexpected of me. They laugh, and say, "Now where's Evelyn going?" God is my best friend, who knows me even better. He just laughs and says, "Here she goes again." In fact, he knows my propensity for boredom and he's constantly changing the scenarios.

*Fourth,* find things that will hold you accountable for the study. Become responsible to someone or something so that you force yourself to continue in the study. Don't let yourself slip into doing nothing. (It's definitely easier.) Listen to tapes in the car. (Books take too much time and energy, I know.) Find someone who needs to be mentored, and make it your goal—then take him or her through a book of the Bible. You'll learn as much from them as they do from you. Learn a new Scripture song each month. Tape stuff to your mirror or the refrigerator door so that you're reminded of who God is to you.

Good, practical advice, Evelyn!

Gary Thomas says, "It is not unusual for the contemplative to be misunderstood and judged by others. . . . But to God, the contemplative's worship is cherished, valued, and rewarded."[20]

The story is told of St. Sarapion the Sindonite, a Desert Father of fourth-century Egypt. He traveled once on a pilgrimage to Rome. There he was told of a celebrated recluse, a woman who lived always in one small room, never going out. Skeptical about her way of life, for he was himself a great wanderer, Sarapion called on her and asked, "Why are you sitting here?" To this she replied, "I am not sitting. I am on a journey."[21] To all the other personalities, the Peaceful Phlegmatic may appear to be "sitting there," when, indeed, they are on a spiritual pilgrimage. Remember, no matter what others may be doing around you, you are on a journey. Let that journey lead you to a closer relationship and deeper knowledge of your Lord.

# Come As You Are

# 9

*Let everyone be sure that he is doing his very best, for then he will have the personal satisfaction of work well done, and won't need to compare himself with someone else.* Galatians 6:4 TLB

When we first began to conceptualize the ideas that turned into this book, we thought we had a good thing going. As we talked through our varied viewpoints and chatted with others, we got very excited about it. Actually, we were unaware of how much need there was. As we gathered stories through our surveys and via our e-mail contacts, we were amazed at the level of response we got from those who contributed. We were surprised not only at the number of respondents, but the passion their stories expressed. We shared the rough drafts with some of these contributors, and their enthusiasm was a great affirmation for us and helped us to know that this book was not just another nice idea. We trust we have been led by the Holy Spirit in our endeavor.

You may have just finished reading the chapter on the personality most applicable to you. While every aspect of each personality has not applied to you—we are all unique—you should have felt at home as you read about others who share your basic personality. Knowing that you are not the only one who feels or responds the way you do should be a freeing experience. That is certainly one of our goals. We hope you shared Jeanne Larson's feelings:

> It helped to know that my struggles are not due to my faultiness, lack of commitment, knowledge deficit, or any of the above, but that the feelings I have are shared by many others and are "normal" for who God made us to be. I think knowing that helps me to be at peace with it and, as you said, "relax," and accept that God loves me for who I am, that I don't have to get it perfect for him, but he understands why I try so hard.

Or as another reader said, "At least I know I am not alone." We hope as you continue to review and ponder the contents of this book that you will feel a new freedom in who God made you to be and also have a better understanding of why others are as God made them to be. As Pam Christian said, "I am greatly freed up to learn that I am not the only one who doesn't get up at 5:00 A.M. to do devotions, pray, and journal every single day. I am most pleased to learn that many other Perfect Melancholies are not all so perfect when it comes to the practical daily discipline of devotion."

Where did we all get this idea? Somehow a standard has been established that sounds wonderful and lofty, but certainly does not fit everyone! We want you to feel the freedom to experiment with what works for you. Trying the things that have worked for others of your personality type is a great place to start. Let go of the standard system that you thought you had to fit into, and relate to God through the way he made you. Forget the "rules." Julia told us, "I've always wondered why my relationship with God seems so strong even though I don't follow the one-hour-with-the-Bible-in-the-prayer-closet-every-morning prescription. When I am in a group of people, and they begin talking about their time with God, I usually remain silent because it always seems that I am breaking some kind of rule in the way I relate to God." Remember, God is there for us, no matter how we come to him! It is not through the rules that we are accepted but through our relationship with Jesus Christ. Come as you are! "For it was through reading the Scripture that I came to realize that I could never find God's favor by trying—and failing—to obey the laws. I came to realize that acceptance with God comes by believing in Christ" (Gal. 2:19 TLB).

We hope that as you read the chapter describing your personality type, you were able to let go of the false guilt that you or others may have unknowingly heaped upon you. Suzy Reynolds said, "In the past I have 'beaten myself up' when I didn't live up to my self-imposed standard. I felt like a failure. Well, now I realize that God's objectives will be accomplished as I yield control to him. The ones that did not go as I intended were not his will. I can let go of the false guilt!"

Many of you grew up with a form of legalism that you are now having to address as an adult. We trust you will be able to let go of the rigidity and find freedom in your relationship with Christ. Brad Huddleston has worked to learn to accept God's grace:

> I can relate so well with the others that you quoted and wrote about. I appreciate their transparency. The Lord has so mercifully helped me break a lot of the legalism that we Perfect Melancholies often experience. It took a bout with depression, but I finally came to the point that I either had to accept his grace or lose my mind. I am happy to report that I chose his grace. I still have to fight legalism at times, but he has helped me so much.

Another reader wrote,

I'm trying to be less regimented in my devotional time with God, to focus on him more than my circumstances, and to listen more. It is taking time to adjust. My prayer time has gotten too introspective. Griping, even to God, still isn't good. Like a typical Perfect Melancholy, I can easily focus on what is wrong. Even my work as an editor gears me to seek out mistakes and correct them. Your chapter was an encouragement and a confirmation to keep going in that direction.

Of course, one drawback to all this knowledge about our personality types is the tendency to use the way we are made as an excuse for sin. We need to take an honest look at our weaknesses and confess to the Lord where we have failed and even sinned. Linda Jewell told us, "For me, understanding my personality has been liberating because I did see that my weaknesses were sins. [Understand that a weakness is not a sin, but may cause us to become lax and allow sin to enter or take control.] During the CLASSeminar, I asked for God's forgiveness for each and every weakness that I had checked. God is so good, for he freed me from believing the lies I believed that I couldn't or didn't have to change." We need to be responsible to grow and gain victory over our faults. As Suzy Ryan found, we may even see some of our past as a step of growth:

Sometimes I feel that my childhood full of adversity is a curse, but after reading my chapter, I now think differently. I realize that this is the avenue God in his grace used to train me to cleave to him. He tempered my personality, allowing me victory over many of the faults of the Popular Sanguine. I knew this prior to reading the chapter, but the words helped all the pieces of the puzzle fit together.

For your personal relationship with God, we hope you receive a new freedom to use the personality God gave you—that you can express your love to him in a way that is natural for you, that you will let go of the guilt you may have felt because you did not measure up to the standards you believed you should have, and that you will use this knowledge to grow beyond the limitations of your personality. Pam Bianco told us,

> It's great to know that my worship style isn't wrong! Being reminded that God made each personality and each style helped me to realize that I can be who God created me to be—rather than forcing myself into how others think I should be! However, knowing my inherent weaknesses allows me to focus not on changing them, but on worshiping in spite of them. It also keeps me from leaning on my weaknesses, and instead to grow beyond them!

Hopefully, you have also read about the other personality types as well as your own. If you have not done so, please do. As you learn about the personalities of others and how the way they are made causes them to seek spirituality in a different way, your acceptance of others will grow. As Pam Christian said, "Reading this book has helped me have even greater appreciation for our differences. The very fact that we are different, yet as believers in Jesus Christ unified, only provides proof that God is supernaturally at work in human hearts."

It is our desire that this book give you an appreciation for and an acceptance of the differences in others' approach to God, that you do not judge them because they may not do exactly the same things you do. Wouldn't it be great if in all our churches we could accept every other type person rather than try to find a church full of people just like us? If your church doesn't cater to a person of your personality, remember, that is what your personal quiet time is all about. A church is made up of all kinds of personalities. We must all be careful not to push too hard for what we need and, in turn, to accept the fact that others have needs, too.

Maxine Holmgren said, "As a Powerful Choleric, I often feel guilty that my times with the Lord are usually not the long, emotional times that some have." While we desire that individuals like Maxine feel released from making the comparison, it is equally important that we accept others as they are. Tami Hay added, "I continue to be amazed at how often all of us at one time or another have looked at someone different from us and out of ignorance criticized them for not doing things the way we do them! Instead of celebrating our differences, we condemn one another. I believe your book will truly be enlightening and freeing for a lot of people."

These differences are especially important to recognize in our homes, with our spouses and children. It is our natural tendency to assume that what works for us will work for others. If they would just do it our way, they would see that it works! However, when our spouse has a different personality, which is almost always the case, his or her spirituality will be manifested in a different way. After reading about her personality and that of her husband, Sheena Fleener wrote us, "I believe many spouses, after reading your book, will understand their mates better when it comes to their relationship with God. The Powerful Choleric in me wants to force my husband to have a disciplined study time because that is what works for me. Thanks for reminding me to shut up and pray!" Sheena's new awareness alone could save marriages! Popular Sanguine/Peaceful Phlegmatic Janet Simcic had a similar discovery:

> My husband is half Popular Sanguine and half Powerful Choleric—but the Powerful Choleric is more at work. Consequently, we do not have devotions together. We are just too distracted! Because I am discipling two gals and am really having fun with it, I tried to tell him that it would be fun for him, too. He disagreed. Since all else failed, I actually threw up a prayer about it. The next week he was invited to join in a prayer group of men who meet on Monday nights. He has "fun," but a Powerful Choleric runs things, so much is accomplished. He said there is a good mix of personalities there to give lots of balance. I love the way we all balance each other. If we would just let ourselves worship

> in our own way at home, and if we who do not have great discipline would stop feeling guilty—wouldn't that be wonderful! Thank you for freeing me!

While your spouse is bound to have a different personality from yours, your children may, as well. Georgia Shaffer found that her Popular Sanguine son was rebelling against his mother's religion because the way her faith was acted out through her Perfect Melancholy personality did not seem to be any fun to him. The structure and discipline was comfortable for her, but not for him. Pamela Christian had a similar experience. She told us this story:

> I have wanted so much for my children to have a personal relationship with Jesus Christ and to provide a home that fully promotes this. With a "mother's heart," I've fretted that my son and daughter are possibly not growing in their faith as sincerely as they should. However, reading this book, I can see how my children are indeed personally relating to God, each in their own way, very real and very personal. Thanks for giving me a tool to better see the truth in my—God's—precious children.

If no one but Pamela gets this concept, the book was worth writing. But we trust that as you read the various sections addressing each personality type, that you, too (assuming you are a parent), see how your children may reach out to God differently. Popular Sanguine Suzy read the Peaceful Phlegmatic chapter and had this response: "This describes my half sister, whom I have judged for not getting more involved in a church or Bible study. I have to let her serve God in her way and release her of my expectations for her Christian life."

Regardless of whether these different people are in your home, your church, or some other aspect of your life, we hope this book will help you to be more accepting and more tolerant of their differences in their search for spirituality. Like Carol John, we believe that understanding each other's differences in the way we relate to God is a tool to help us love one another better. Carol said, "Tolerance is a favorite subject and a popular solution to the problems of mankind. It's the politically correct thing to do, but love is the Christian thing to do. I have been teaching the personalities in the church as a tool to help us love one another better. 'My command is this: Love each other as I have loved you' (John 15:12)."

With the idea of love and acceptance, we especially appreciated Ann Downing's response. Let her prayer be your prayer:

> In the area of acceptance, I'm learning how important it is to understand God's grace extended to us, all of us the same grace, accepting us in our uniqueness. How can we strive for anything less toward our fellow travelers on this journey? We are all special, regardless of our differences, and our prayer should be "Lord, help me to accept the differences as you accept me with my weaknesses as well as my strengths."

We want you to have a sense of freedom in who God made you to be. Each of us needs to be reminded to accept those who are different, as Christ accepted us. Evelyn Jimenez wrote, "The unconditional love of Christ came and accepted us just as we are. We did not have to get our act together before we came to Christ. We did not have to perform to be received into his arms. We just came, and he accepted us without conditions—with a love that has no measure." We can come as we are, and we should offer this same freedom to others.

However, rather than resting in who you are, we want to challenge you to first experience God through the person he made you to be. Then, once you have developed a system or style that works for you, we want to encourage you to move beyond that comfort zone and try new things that can add a new depth and richness to your search for spirituality. Reread the sections on the other personalities. As you read, highlight techniques or tools that different personalities say have worked for them. If there is an approach that is new to you, try it. As you move beyond what is natural for you, you may find something with which you experience God on a whole new level. We can all learn from each other. Georgia Shaffer said, "I believe the power of your book lies in the fact that as we read about ourselves in the quotes and stories of others, it helps us to see the 'truth' in a way in which we are not so defensive—then we are more open to change." You have read about yourself; we hope you will also be open to change, to stretching, and exploring.

Evelyn Jimenez shared the following with us:

> So many times people have tried to put me in a box because of my personality. They felt that if I conformed to their image, the world would be a better place. However, God created the world with a variety of colors and a splendor of differences. These differences were not to compete against each other, but to complement each other in the uniqueness of who God created us to be. We need to be free to be the people God intended us to be. To complement one another like a field of wild flowers that are waving in the wind. All different heights, shapes, and colors—but each unique because we are created by the Master's hand. To be free is to be who God created us to be. Not to be boxed—not allowed to be who we are—but to be opened as a beautiful package to bring glory to our Creator.

As you have the freedom to be who God created you to be, you will blossom. As you give others the acceptance of who they are, they will blossom. Together you will be like that beautiful bouquet of wild flowers, a beautiful package bringing glory to your Creator.

# Final Thoughts

At the University of Chicago Divinity School, each year they have what is called "Baptist Day." It is a day when all the Baptists in the area are invited to the school, because they want the Baptist dollars to keep coming in. On this day, each one is to bring a lunch to be eaten outdoors in a grassy picnic area. And every Baptist Day the school invites one of the greatest minds to lecture in the theological education center. One year they invited Dr. Paul Tillich.

Dr. Tillich spoke for two and a half hours seeking to prove that the resurrection of Jesus Christ was false. He quoted scholar after scholar and book after book. He concluded that since there was no such thing as the historical resurrection, the religious tradition of the church was groundless, emotional mumbo-jumbo, because it was based on a relationship with a risen Jesus who, in fact, never rose from the dead in any literal sense. He then asked if there were any questions.

After about thirty seconds, an old, dark-skinned preacher with a head of short-cropped, woolly white hair stood up in the back of the auditorium. "Docta Tillich, I got one question," he said, as all eyes turned toward him. He reached into his sack lunch and pulled out an apple, and began eating it. "Docta Tillich . . ." *crunch, munch* . . . "My question is a simple question." *crunch, munch* . . . "I don't know nothin' about Niebuhr and Heidegger . . ." *crunch, munch* . . . He finished the apple. "All I wanna know is: this apple I just ate—was it bitter or sweet?"

Dr. Tillich paused for a moment and answered in exemplary scholarly fashion: "I cannot possibly answer that question, for I haven't tasted your apple."

The white-haired preacher dropped the core of his apple into his crumpled paper bag, looked up at Dr. Tillich, and said calmly, "Neither have you tasted my Jesus."

The 1,000 plus in attendance could not contain themselves. The auditorium erupted with applause and cheers. Dr. Tillich thanked his audience and promptly left the platform.[1]

We have talked a lot about the various ways the different personalities have found to "taste Jesus." Psalm 34:8 says, "Taste and see that the Lord is good. Oh, the joys of those who trust in him!"(NLT). There are marvelous benefits to spending time with the Lord.

Because we believe so strongly in the centrality of a personal relationship with Jesus Christ, we have endeavored to find a way to communicate how important it is to spend time getting to know him on a regular basis. We are aware that just reading about the various personalities and the ways that they have found to connect with God is not enough. Now we want to challenge you to make the choice to set aside a regular time to meet with the Lord. 1 Peter 2:2–3 gives us this direction: "You must crave pure spiritual milk so that you can grow into the fullness of your salvation. Cry out for this nourishment as a baby cries for milk, now that you have had a taste of the Lord's kindness" (NLT).

Our desire has been to help you discover the freedom of finding God according to the personality in which he made you. We have striven to break the "mold" of thinking that there is just one "right" way to do devotions. But what we do not want to do is to imply that there is no need for such a time. Relationships are time-consuming. To really get to know a person, we must spend time with him or her. God wants to be known by you. He sent his Son, Jesus, to reveal to us his character. He went to the trouble of finding willing men and women to record his acts in history in order that we might know about him. He will communicate with us through his Word, through prayer, preaching, teaching, music, nature, his still, small voice, and through our friends. But he waits for us to invite him into our most private lives.

A. W. Tozer, in his classic book *The Pursuit of God*, says,

> We have almost forgotten that God is a person and, as such, can be cultivated as any person can. It is inherent in personality to be able to know other personalities, but full knowledge of one personality by another cannot be achieved in one encounter. It is only after long and loving mental intercourse that the full possibilities of both can be explored.
>
> All social intercourse between human beings is a response of personality to personality, grading upward from the most casual brush between man and man to the fullest, most intimate communion of which the human soul is capable. Religion, so far as it is genuine, is in essence the response of created personalities to the creating personality, God.[2]

Our personality responding to the personality of the God who created us . . . unique, special, one of a kind. Our personality, being conformed to his personality, being transformed from the weaknesses inherent in each personality, by the "renewing of our minds" (Rom.

12:2). This is the way to find the real meaning of ourselves.

In *The Screwtape Letters* by C. S. Lewis, the senior devil, Screwtape, is admonishing his underling Wormwood, for allowing his "patient" to actually experience real pleasure. His point is that in order to woo away a "patient" from the "enemy" (God) one must "palm off vanity, bustle, irony, and expensive tedium as pleasures."

> [Real pleasure] would peel off from his sensibility the kind of crust you have been forming on it, and make him feel that he was coming home, recovering himself. As a preliminary to detaching him from the Enemy [God], you wanted to detach him from himself, and had made some progress in doing so. Now all that is undone.
>
> Of course, I know that the Enemy also wants to detach men from themselves, but in a different way. Remember, always, that He really likes the little vermin, and *sets an absurd value on the distinctness of every one of them*. When He talks of their losing their selves, He means only abandoning the clamor of self-will; once they have done that, He really gives them back all their personality, and boasts (I am afraid, sincerely) that when they are wholly His *they will be more themselves than ever*.[3]

We all long to be more than we are, to be all that we can be. We seek fulfillment, with a passion, to fill the emptiness inside. To become fully the personality that God created us to be, we have to give up our self-will to his will. Even Jesus had to do that. He prayed in the Garden on the last night of his life, "My Father! If it is possible, let this cup be taken away from me. But I want your will, not mine" (Matt. 26:39 TLB).

Jesus said in simple terms, "And this is the way to have eternal life—to know you, the only true God, and Jesus Christ, the one you sent to earth" (John 17:3 NLT). Throughout the Scriptures, the passionate burning desire of men and women of the past has been to know God. Moses cried out in Exodus to God, asking to know him and for God to show himself to Moses. God promised, "I will personally go with you, Moses. I will give you rest—everything will be fine for you" (Ex. 33:14 NLT).

The Psalms are full of David's longing to know the Lord, filled with the cry of both the seeker and the ecstasy of one who has found. Paul said the burning desire of his life was "the priceless gain of knowing Christ Jesus my Lord. . . . As a result, I can really know Christ and experience the mighty power that raised him from the dead" (Phil. 3:8, 10 NLT).

All of these became fully who they were created to be as they grew in intimate knowledge of the God who created them and called them. Then they stepped out in ministry with authority. Again, Jesus is our example. Charles Kraft, author of *Deep Wounds, Deep Healing,* speaks of this when he states, "I believe our spiritual authority flows directly from our intimacy with Jesus. . . . We should, therefore, do our best to imitate Jesus' approach to maintaining intimacy with the Father. Though he was a Son, he worked at the Father-Son relationship by regularly spending time with the Father."[4]

Getting to know him in a personal relationship that grows daily is the purpose behind this book. The various methods given are only suggestions to help you find the way to connect with God and begin this lifelong journey of discovery. Discovery about him, his character, his desires for us, his plans, and his ways. God is a Being, who thinks, wills, enjoys, feels, loves, desires, and suffers. In making himself known to us, he uses personality. He communicates with us through our minds, our wills, and our emotions. He desires to interact with us on the most mundane level of our life. He also desires to lift us into higher places where we can view and understand the dailiness of life from his perspective. He wants to not only reveal himself to us in all his glory but to reveal to us how he sees us and who he calls us to become. The Scriptures are full of his longings for us. He compares himself to a mother hen: "How often I have wanted to gather your children together as a hen protects her chicks beneath her wings, but you wouldn't let me" (Matt. 23:37 NLT). He tells us that as a shepherd looks for his lost sheep, he searches for us. Like a gardener who prunes for better crops, he tenderly watches our growth. He waits patiently for us to seek him and promises that in our seeking we shall find him. He longs to meet with us, but we have to be willing to meet with him.

A Sunday school teacher related to me an exercise she had recently done with her class of first graders. Each child was given toothpicks and craft sticks and told to make a picture from these simple tools, gluing them on paper to depict one of God's characteristics. Their imaginations ran wild as they designed their own special depictions of God. Upon completion, each child was given another plain piece of paper, which was placed directly on top of the raised design. They were then instructed to take a crayon and rub it back and forth over the plain paper. As they did, the impression beneath came through clearly, transferring the image from the bottom to the top.

"The top paper symbolizes you, and when you draw close to God, and life rubs you, God's character is what shows through," they were told. So, too, is our life. What we show to the world on a daily basis is what is inside of us. In order for God's character to be revealed, we must know him well.

To know him means establishing a personal relationship, becoming intimate with him, spending time with him, learning, listening, observing, and trusting. Most of you reading this book have already invited God, through Jesus Christ, into your heart and life. But he may only be there as a casual acquaintance who has dropped by to visit. He wants to be so much more to you than this. He wants you to know him with all that he has to offer, that in whatever circumstance you find yourself, you will never be alone; you will never need to fear. Getting to know him takes time and effort, as does the establishment of any meaningful relationship. A quick "hi" in passing to a person does not establish relationship. An occasional meal or a few minutes of conversation does not reveal a person's true self. It is the continued contact over time, when things are going well and when they are not, that forges the bonds and ties that give us the freedom to trust and finally to love. It is a desire that demands a choice on our part to begin. It will mean a shift in priorities. Our schedules will have to be adjusted. Decisions will need to be made.

Many of us may relate to the woman at the well as seen in John 4. She came seeking water to quench her thirst. When Jesus offered her "living water" that "takes away thirst altogether," she jumped at his offer. Seeing something that would instantly answer her permanent problem of needing to come daily to the well, she greedily grasped for it. But Jesus was offering something far beyond her immediate need. He offered to reveal who she really was. But his offer demanded more of her than she was ready to give. Perhaps thinking to distract the Lord, she tried to conceal her greed by challenging his authority. He only reiterated his initial offer, the living water—himself—the Messiah! And in that moment she saw all that she ever was—and the one who loved and accepted her anyway.

Jesus offers to show us all that we have ever been and then in loving tenderness to walk with us daily, molding us into all that he created us to be. Will you accept his invitation? He graciously invites, and waits, never intruding into our freedoms. He has given us a choice, and he will not violate this. It's a choice with a guarantee. He holds out the benefits, offers the gifts, but never forces our response. His choice was to create us with a free will, to let us make our own decisions. He wants to spend time with us, he eagerly awaits our coming to him, but he will never MAKE us do so. He looks for ways to draw us to him, and those ways are suited to our unique personality. He knows the demands of our life, the time pressures and the responsibilities, and he desires to lighten our daily load by carrying our burdens for us. Jesus said, "Come to me, all of you who are weary and carry heavy burdens, and I will give you rest. Take my yoke upon you. Let me teach you, because I am humble and gentle, and you will find rest for your souls. For my yoke fits perfectly, and the burden I give you is light" (Matt. 11:28–30 NLT).

## The Choice to Come Is Ours!

You have seen illustrated by the stories throughout this book the various ways that God has met each person. God has his own special plan for you, too. We encourage you to keep trying different ways until you find the ones that work the best for you. This may change in different periods of your life. We pray that this book will open the door to new possibilities and ideas that will encourage you in choosing to spend time getting to know him, the one who created you and loves you.

# Notes

## Chapter 1

1. Henry T. Blackaby and Claude V. King, *Experiencing God: Knowing and Doing the Will of God* (Nashville: Broadman, 1994).
2. *Self* (Dec. 1997).
3. *Wall Street Journal* (Dec. 24, 1997).
4. *Context* (Oct. 15, 1997).

## Chapter 2

1. As told by Richard Foster.
2. *Christianity Today* (July 1996).
3. *Los Angeles Times*.

## Chapter 3

1. George Howe Colt, "Were You Born That Way?" *Life* (Apr. 1998): 40.
2. Summaries adapted from the *Life Application Bible*'s Personality Profile.
3. All three of these titles were written by Florence Littauer and Marita Littauer, and are available by calling (800) 433-6633.

## Chapter 4

1. *The Personality Profile* was created by Fred Littauer and is taken from Florence Littauer, *After Every Wedding Comes a Marriage* (Eugene, Ore: Harvest House Publishers, 1981). Used by permission. Not to be duplicated. Additional copies may be ordered by calling (800) 433-6633.

## Chapter 5

1. Henri Nouwen, *Out of Solitude* (Notre Dame, Ind.: Ave Maria Press, 1974), 14.

## Chapter 6

1. Article by Michael J. Gerson, *U.S. News and World Report* (May 4, 1998): 20–29.
2. Gary Thomas, *Sacred Pathways* (Nashville: Thomas Nelson Publishers, 1996), 142–3.
3. Bill Hybels, *The God You're Looking For* (Nashville: Thomas Nelson Publishers, 1997), 4.
4. *Life Application Bible* (Wheaton, Ill.: Tyndale House Publishers, 1988), 71.
5. Jean Fleming, *Finding Focus in a Whirlwind World* (Dallas: Roper Press, 1991), 73.
6. Henri Nouwen, *Reaching Out* (New York: Doubleday, 1975), 146.
7. John 5:19; 8:26–28; 12:49–50; 14:10.
8. Dallas Willard, *The Spirit of the Disciplines* (San Francisco: Harper & Row, 1988), 161.
9. Richard Foster, *Celebration of Discipline* (San Francisco: Harper & Row, 1988), 96.
10. Fred Smith, "Conducting a Spiritual Audit," LEADERSHIP magazine (Winter 1998): 45.
11. O. Hallesby, *Temperament and the Christian Faith* (Minneapolis: Augsburg Publishing House, 1962), 77.

## Chapter 7

1. Georgia Shaffer, York, PA
2. Irene Carloni, Manhattan Beach, CA
3. Barbara Anson, Tracy, CA
4. Becky Gilkerson, Apple Valley, CA

5. Oswald Chambers, *My Utmost for His Highest,* May 12 entry (Westwood, N.J.: Barbour Books, 1987).
6. Mark Reed, *Decision* magazine (January 1997): 7.
7. Marjorie Lee Chandler, Solvang, CA
8. Robert Schuller, *God's Minute,* Jan. 7 entry.
9. Oswald Chambers, *My Utmost for His Highest,* Feb. 23 entry.
10. Jo Franz, Fresno, CA
11. Diana James, Meridan, ID
12. Marianne Lambert, Colorado Springs, CO
13. Pat Daily, Oakland, ME
14. Katheryn Haddad, Woodslee, ONT
15. Kenton Beshore, Pastor, Mariners South Coast Community Church, Irvine, CA
16. As quoted by Richard Foster, *Theology News & Notes,* Fuller Seminary, Oct. 1982.
17. Joan Mcgrady-Beach, Reinbeck, IA
18. LEADERSHIP magazine, dialogue with Richard Foster & Henri Nouwen (Winter Quarter 1982).
19. Steven Curtis Chapman, *Focus on the Family* magazine (Apr. 1997).
20. Jack Deere, "God, Are You There?" *Charisma* (Sept. 1996): 54–48.
21. Cathy Lynn Grossman, cover story, inset box, *USA Today,* May 27, 1998.
22. Connie Witt, Lincoln, NE
23. Becky Thompson, Mesa, AZ
24. Jeanne Larsen, Lodi, CA
25. LouElla Dryer, Tempe, AZ
26. Shelly Albany, Yorba Linda, CA

## Chapter 8

1. Anne Greer, Santa Ana, CA
2. Dr. Jerry Ozee, Sullivan, IL

3. Evelyn Sloat, Denver, PA
4. Ken Klassen, Tampa, FL
5. Sue Roberts, Orlando, FL
6. Kathy Johnston, Miramar, FL
7. *Sacred Pathways*.
8. Dietrich Bonhoeffer, *Letters & Papers From Prison* (New York: The Macmillan Company, 1981).
9. Craig Brian Larson, LEADERSHIP magazine (Winter 1998): 52.
10. Chuck Alt, Mt. Pulaski, MI
11. Ceanne Richards, Luling, TX
12. Barbara Amavisca, Placentia, CA
13. Suzzi Marquis, Tustin, CA
14. Ceil Sharman, Laguna Beach, CA
15. Judy Nill, "Praying the Scriptures," *Presbyterians Today* (Mar. 1998): 88:2, 18–19.
16. Beverly Stone, Richardson, TX
17. Elizabeth Carlson, *Decision* magazine (June 1997): 15.
18. *Temperament and the Christian Faith*, 94–95.
19. Ibid., 92–96.
20. *Sacred Pathways.*
21. Told by Fr. Kallistos Ware in *The Orthodox Way* (St. Vladmirs, 1979), 7.

## Final Thoughts

1. Frank Ifuku, quoted on the Internet, received through e-mail.
2. A. W. Tozer, *The Pursuit of God* (Camp Hill, Penn.: Christian Literature Crusade, 1982), 13.
3. C. S. Lewis, *The Screwtape Letters* (New York: The Macmillan Company, 1970), 59.
4. Charles H. Kraft, *Deep Wounds, Deep Healing* (Ann Arbor, Mich.: Servant Publications, 1993), 30.

***Thank you for selecting a book from***
**BETHANY HOUSE PUBLISHERS**

Bethany House Publishers is a ministry of Bethany Fellowship International, an interdenominational, nonprofit organization committed to spreading the Good News of Jesus Christ around the world through evangelism, church planting, literature distribution, and care for those in need. Missionary training is offered through Bethany College of Missions.

Bethany Fellowship International is a member of the National Association of Evangelicals and subscribes to its statement of faith. If you would like further information, please contact:

Bethany Fellowship International
6820 Auto Club Road
Minneapolis, MN 55438 USA